NIFTY™

Clean & Organized

MONEY-SAVING HACKS and EASY DIYs for a Clean and Clutter-Free Home!

Money-Saving Tips

Small Space Hacks

Projects You Can Make

ADAMS MEDIA
NEW YORK LONDON TORONTO SYDNEY NEW DELHI

Adams Media
An Imprint of Simon & Schuster, Inc.
100 Technology Center Drive
Stoughton, Massachusetts 02072

First Adams Media hardcover edition November 2021

ADAMS MEDIA and colophon are trademarks of Simon & Schuster.

NIFTY is a trademark of BuzzFeed, Inc., and used under license. All rights reserved.

For information about special discounts for bulk purchases, please contact Simon & Schuster Special Sales at 1-866-506-1949 or business@simonandschuster.com.

The Simon & Schuster Speakers Bureau can bring authors to your live event. For more information or to book an event contact the Simon & Schuster Speakers Bureau at 1-866-248-3049 or visit our website at www.simonspeakers.com.

Interior design by Sylvia McArdle
Photographs © Getty Images; 123RF; BuzzFeed, Inc.
Illustrations by Alaya Howard

Manufactured in the United States of America

1 2021

Library of Congress Cataloging-in-Publication Data
Title: Nifty™: clean & organized
Other titles: Nifty (Website)
Description: First Adams Media hardcover edition. | Stoughton, MA: Adams Media, 2021
Identifiers: LCCN 2021018951 | ISBN 9781507216002 (hc) | ISBN 9781507216019 (ebook)
Subjects: LCSH: House cleaning. | Storage in the home. | Orderliness.
Classification: LCC TX324 .N54 2021 | DDC 648/.5--dc23
LC record available at https://lccn.loc.gov/2021018951

ISBN 978-1-5072-1600-2
ISBN 978-1-5072-1601-9 (ebook)

Contents

Introduction

There are two kinds of people: those who love to fold clean clothes and declutter the junk drawer and those who'd rather do just about anything else. If you're reading this book because you're in the first group and want tips to take your cleaning to the next level, you're in the right place. And if you're in the second group and you're hoping for some hacks to make cleaning faster and easier—so you can just be *done* with it already!—you've come to the right place too.

The following chapters cover every room in your home, from the kitchen to the bedroom to the living room to the bathroom to the garage. Whether you need to organize your office, dust your dining room, or sort your laundry, you'll find practical advice, simple tips, and step-by-step DIY projects to make the process easy. Along the way, we'll focus on cutting clutter (do you *really* need twenty coffee mugs?!) and finding creative ways to make the most of the space you have (embrace floor pillows instead of bulky furniture). The ideas and projects in this book don't need to be followed to the letter—instead, look to them as inspiration and feel free to personalize them to fit your preferences and home. To easily find ideas that you need, watch for icons that call out hacks that are:

| Perfect for small spaces | Just right if you're handy with basic tools | Ideal for kids' stuff | Best for seasonal use | Able to save you money | Designed to clean and organize your pets' gear |

Whether you rent a studio apartment or own a spacious house with a yard; whether you live alone, with roommates, or with family; and whether you love household chores or hate them, you'll definitely appreciate the rewards of living in a clean and organized space. When you reduce your kitchen appliance collection so your cabinets aren't overfilled, use nontoxic bathroom cleaners that don't give you a headache, and open a closet to find a neat row of hangers instead of a tangle of clothes, you'll discover that you can find what you need faster, spend less time cleaning, and enjoy your space so much more.

Get ready to spend less time doing housework and more time living your life!

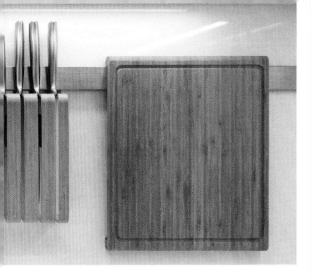

Kitchen
No Room to Be Messy

You cook here. You snack here. You wander in here when you have no real reason to be here, just because it's the kitchen. The **kitchen** has a way of becoming the center of any home—and that's why keeping it clean and **organized** is so important.

Make Your Kitchen Inviting

You'll be more likely to maintain a clean and organized space if you enjoy being in that room to begin with, so prioritize making your kitchen comfortable and aesthetically pleasing. If your chairs are uncomfortable, upgrade them when your budget allows. Hang wall decor that makes you happy. Many simple, affordable touches like these can make your kitchen a place you *want* to keep clean.

Give Everything a Home

A large part of cleaning and organizing actually just involves returning household items to their proper place. Shoes, small tools like screwdrivers, and mail might end up in the kitchen, but they probably don't belong there. Designate a home for everything and you'll find that tidying up becomes much easier.

Make Cooking Convenient

One thing that makes for a frustrating cooking experience is having to repeatedly go back and forth to grab the spatula, the slotted spoon, the oven mitts, and everything else you need. Store frequently used items near the stove to cut down on all that scurrying.

Don't Buy All the Things

There are so many shiny kitchen items out there, from appliances and gadgets to utensils and serving pieces. And it can be very tempting—especially when you're browsing a gorgeous website or cute local kitchen store—to buy one of each.

But the vast majority of people don't need—and won't end up using—all those fancy contraptions. They'll become objects that exist simply to be organized and cleaned. And that's a waste of time, space, and money.

Before you buy—or acquire for free—any new kitchen item, ask yourself: Is this really solving a problem or meeting a need? Will it make my life better or easier? Will its benefit to me balance out my responsibility to store and clean it?

You may find that simply avoiding unnecessary additions makes cleaning and organizing your kitchen effortlessly easier.

Store Like with Like Using Zones

If all your things hang out with similar things, you'll never find yourself searching for a particular item. Need a mug? It's on the mug shelf. Need a cleaner? It's with all the other cleaning supplies! Need a pen? You get the idea. Storing items according to their function—such as baking, food prep, or storage—will ensure that everything you need for a given task or meal is all in one place when you need it.

This is especially useful in high-traffic spaces, like your fridge or pantry. Organizing those spaces is not a one-and-done project; things are still going to get messy sometimes. But it's much easier to nip that mess in the bud when you know that the milk cartons always live on the top shelf of the fridge and the Tupperware containers go on the left side of the bottom cupboard. Once you establish your zones, you'll know where to put new items away and where to look when you need some sugar.

Reclaim Your Kitchen Countertops

If your countertops are cluttered, try one of these creative solutions:

• Lean a decorative wooden ladder against a wall in or just outside your kitchen. Hang two S-hooks from each rung, then hang another S-hook from each initial hook. Slide these doubled hooks into the handles of rectangular woven or wire baskets. Now you have multiple places besides your counter to keep fruit, jars, or other necessities.

- Put a three-tiered lazy Susan or dessert stand on the counter to stash three times the amount of spice jars, tea tins, or other small items that were previously taking up too much space when spread out.

- Place a shelf—either a portable shelf supported on legs or a shelf attached to the wall—on or above your countertop to create two levels of horizontal surface instead of one.

- Affix a peg rack to the wall and hang mugs from their handles; taking them off a shelf frees up shelf space for some of your countertop items.

Reclaim Unused Space with Adhesive Hooks

When you're tight on space, you want to maximize every inch. And the MVP of making the most when you have the least is adhesive hooks. They are easy to use, don't damage walls, and are super sturdy. Buy an inexpensive pack, remove the backing, and start sticking. Here are four ways to transform your kitchen using hooks:

1. Straighten out your baking supplies. Don't waste precious drawer space on measuring cups and spoons. Instead, attach a few hooks to the inside door of the cabinet where you keep your flour, sugar, and other dry ingredients. Then hang your measuring utensils right there within reach of what you're measuring.

2. Organize your pot lids. Stick hooks on the inside door of the cabinet where you keep your pots, and hang lids from them. This opens up space within the cabinet while keeping lids close to their pot partners.

3. Decorate with your cookware. Who needs useless decorative items? Save time and money by adhering some hooks to your kitchen wall and hanging your favorite colanders, colorful pots, and other interesting pieces. This not only displays your most interesting cookware, but it frees up a ton of cabinet and counter space.

4. Create your own foil, parchment paper, plastic wrap, and/or wax paper dispensers. On the inside door of a cabinet, adhere two hooks at a distance slightly greater than the length of your box. Insert a dowel through the box's perforated holes and the cardboard roll itself (if the packaging doesn't have perforated holes, you can make your own with scissors) and rest it on the hooks.

5 Amazing Uses for Baking Soda

You might have noticed that lots of the cleaning tips in this chapter involve baking soda. That's because this everyday product, also known as bicarbonate of soda, is truly a miracle worker in the kitchen. Here are some easy hacks using this common ingredient:

1. Deep-clean your stovetop. Mix 1 cup of baking soda with ½ cup of water and a dash of citrus essential oil. Soak paper towels in the mixture and carefully place around the heating elements to soften grime, then add more of the mixture and scrub with the scrubbing side of a sponge as needed.

2. Keep your fridge smelling fresh. Place an open box of baking soda inside it. Change it out every month or so.

3. Absorb garbage odors. Sprinkle some baking soda inside your kitchen garbage can—or just place an open box of baking soda at the bottom of the can to make replacing it easier.

4. Unclog a sluggish kitchen sink drain. Pour in a pot of boiling water, then ½ cup of baking soda. Wait for 5 minutes, then pour in 1 cup of hot water mixed with 1 cup of white vinegar. Wait for 10 minutes, then pour in a second pot of boiling water.

5. Put out minor cooking fires. Your kitchen should absolutely be equipped with a real fire extinguisher, and you don't want to mess around with flames, so call the fire department if need be! However, a handy fact to remember in a pinch is that pouring baking soda on a small grease or oil fire can smother it.

Give Your Sink a Nightly Scrub

Mixing up this simple scrub and giving your sink a quick cleaning before you head to bed every night will keep your sink spotless. To make the scrub, combine 2 cups of baking soda, 10 drops of lemon essential oil, 10 drops of clove essential oil, and 1 squirt of dish soap in a glass jar or plastic container.

To clean the sink, wet it. Sprinkle $\frac{1}{4}$ cup of the baking soda mixture in the sink. Add a squirt of dish soap in the sink and scrub with a scrub brush. Rinse and dry with a cloth. Store the rest of the scrub in a cool, dark place for up to six months.

Get Rid of Annoying Kitchen Stains

These little kitchen tricks will help you conquer the most irksome of stains:

- To clean **yellowed plastic containers**, rub half a lemon over the surface. Place the container in direct sunlight for a day or two. The stains will fade or even disappear.

- To clean **discoloration on a wooden cutting board**, sprinkle baking soda over the stain, then scrub with half a lemon. Once the stains fade, wipe with a towel.

- To clean **a coffee- or tea-stained mug**, apply white toothpaste to the stain. Gently scrub with a toothbrush and let sit for about 10 minutes. Wash with warm water.

- To clean **hard-water stains from silverware and glassware**, cut a grapefruit in half. Sprinkle salt on the grapefruit halves and use them to polish utensils and glasses. Rinse clean.

Restore Your Pots & Pans to Their Shining Glory

Cooking is messy. Here are some tricks, using natural ingredients you have in your kitchen, for dealing with the aftermath:

1. The burned exterior of a stainless steel pan: Sprinkle baking soda over the stained areas. Slowly pour white vinegar on top of the baking soda. The ingredients will combine to form a paste. Let sit for 30 minutes, or longer for more severe stains. Crumple a piece of aluminum foil into a ball and gently scrub the pan. Rinse and rewash when stains are gone.

2. Burned food from the inside of a pan: Fill the pan with equal parts water and white vinegar. Bring the mixture to a boil. Pour out the liquid, then scrub the pan with a soft sponge. The softened residue should come off easily.

3. A scorched pan: Fill with 1 cup of water, then add 1 tablespoon of cream of tartar and stir. Bring to a simmer, then let cool. Clean with the scrubbing side of a sponge. Rinse clean. If any residue remains, sprinkle on more cream of tartar, add a little warm water, and keep scrubbing.

4. Burned food from the inner pot of a slow cooker: Fill with water, then add 1 cup of white vinegar and 1 cup of baking soda. Put on the lid, turn to high, and simmer for 1 hour. Unplug and rinse out. Wipe clean with a paper towel.

5. Burned spills inside the slow cooker base: Stir water and baking soda into a paste, then spread on the affected areas and let dry. Dip a scrub brush in white vinegar and scrub, then wipe with a paper towel. Repeat if needed.

7 Areas to Remember to Clean in Your Kitchen

There's more to kitchen cleaning than wiping countertops—dirt and dust can hide in plenty of other areas too. The next time you clean the kitchen, don't neglect these spots:

1. Walls: No place in a kitchen is safe from little splashes and stains.

2. The tops of the fridge door and dishwasher door: You'll wonder how they even got dirty, but you'll be glad you cleaned them.

3. All of your stovetop: It's not enough to wipe up obvious spills. To really clean your gas stovetop, remove the grates and clean underneath them. Electric stovetops can be cleaned the same way, by removing the heating coils—just make sure they're fully cooled first! And while you're at it, wipe down the oven door handle.

4. Inside the fridge and freezer: In addition to clearing out old food, wash the shelves and walls of your fridge and freezer, including inside the crisper and other compartments.

5. Kitchen curtains: Kitchen curtains should be washed regularly just like other linens. Newly washed and ironed curtains will make your kitchen look and feel much fresher.

6. Under the sink: "Out of sight, out of mind" really applies here. Unfortunately, not only can this spot get cluttered, but you might be unaware of a spilled bottle or leaking pipe.

7. Garbage can: Inside, outside, all of it. And the floor under it. If possible, clean your garbage can outside with a hose. If that's not possible, put the can in your shower stall and clean it in there.

Clean Your Microwave Naturally in Seconds

Microwaves can get pretty nasty pretty quickly. But the remedy doesn't have to include a harsh cleanser or vigorous scrubbing. Here's an extremely simple, all-natural way to clean your microwave using its own heat. Slice 2 lemons and place the slices in a microwave-safe bowl filled halfway with water. Put the bowl in the microwave, then heat it until the water boils. Carefully remove the bowl with oven mitts. Wipe away the now-softened grime inside the microwave with a sponge.

Clean As You Go

If you quickly wipe down counters and other frequently used kitchen surfaces each time you use them, you'll rarely have to do a massive full-kitchen scrubbing. This tactic won't entirely eliminate the need for more in-depth cleaning sessions, but it will help make that regular chore easier and faster.

Make Your Own Under-the-Cabinet Spice Rack

Looking for the perfect place to store your spices when you need them in a pinch? This super simple DIY puts them right where you need them: above the counter where you do your prep. Now a sprinkle of sea salt is always within reach. Win!

WHAT YOU NEED:

- 4 (4-ounce) Mason jars (make sure the lids contain enough metal to be magnetized)
- Drill and drill bits or screwdriver
- 1 (12-inch) steel bracket
- 6 ($\frac{1}{4}$-inch) wood screws
- 6 round magnets (2 inches in diameter)

HOW TO DO IT:

1. Label the jars in whatever style you like. Fill them with your favorite spices and secure the lids.

2. Using a drill or screwdriver, mount the steel bracket to the underside of your cabinet, over your countertop, with the wood screws. Space out the screws every 2 inches.

3. Place the magnets on the steel bracket, lining them up directly next to one another. The magnets should run the full length of the bracket.

4. Starting from the right, connect the spice-filled Mason jars to the magnets one at a time. Each jar should need only about one and a half magnets, letting you fit all four jars on the six magnets.

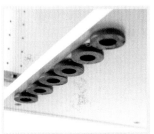

5 *Multitasking Kitchen Items That Save Space*

If you don't have room for everything you think your kitchen needs, don't worry. A lot of common kitchen items do double, triple, or even quadruple duty! These kitchen standbys might be more useful than you realize:

1. Wet/dry mop: It mops the floor and dusts the ceiling and walls, and some models can be lengthened or shortened as the task demands. (Plus, it can be used to coax out-of-reach items from under the fridge or the back of the shelf.)

2. Nice measuring cups: All measuring cups measure, but aesthetically pleasing ones can also be used as small serving bowls or even decorations.

3. Tea towels: They look pretty, but they also mop up spills, dry dishes, protect you from hot pans, and moonlight as placemats.

4. Rubber gloves: They might be meant for washing dishes, but they stand in quite nicely for jar openers too.

5. Blender: It seems everyone has separate appliances for smoothies, soups, and sauces. But you can make all of these—plus crush ice, make purees, and turn grains to flour or bread crumbs—with an old-fashioned blender.

Let Open Shelving Keep You in Line

Imagine if all your plates, glassware, canned food, and everything else in your kitchen cabinets were suddenly visible to anyone who entered the room. Would you be embarrassed by the amount of stuff you own or the unsightly state of your shelves? That realization might motivate you to keep your shelving clean and organized.

That's why one ruthless but ultimately helpful (and aesthetically pleasing!) solution is open kitchen shelving. Whether you're renovating a kitchen or moving into a place with existing open shelves, this design feature can really force you to get clean, organized, and coordinated.

This method can also help you reduce excess buying by giving you a clearer picture of how much you can store.

Give Awkward Spaces a Glow-Up

In difficult-to-reach corners and deep cabinets, a lazy Susan (or rotating tray) will let you spin your spices around until the one you need is at your fingertips. If your baking sheets extend beyond your shelves, store them vertically in tiny in-between spaces, such as between the fridge and the end of the counter. For extra-high shelves, use a step stool or buy a grabber (aka a reacher), a lightweight tool that hardly takes up any space in a closet.

Carve Out a Spot for Your Pets

If you have a cat or dog, you probably store, prepare, and serve their food in the kitchen...all of which can lead to a sticky floor situation. Here's how to bring some order to your pets' chaotic little corner of the kitchen:

• **Give pets their own zone.** If you have the space, devote a cabinet or shelf entirely to your pet's food, treats, extra bowls and mats, and so on. If you don't have shelf space for all those cans, use a cute container the size of a small trash can to hold it all.

• **Store dry food in plastic cereal containers.** They're sleeker and easier to pour from, and they keep food fresh longer than bulky paper bags. And bonus: Your pet can't shred them in search of snacks. Large glass jars or metal tins with measuring scoops work too.

• **Anticipate messes.** Put a large placemat made of an easy-to-wipe material under food and water bowls.

• **Take advantage of your dishwasher.** You're probably already cleaning your pet's food dishes there, but you can also add most hard plastic or rubber toys and synthetic collars and leashes to the load. Just use white vinegar instead of detergent.

Get a Handle on Your Reusable Bag Mess

If you, like most people, own dozens of reusable shopping bags, select the most attractive of the bunch and use it as a storage bag for the others. Hang it over a doorknob or hook and it becomes kitchen decor and a practical organization solution in one.

Add Space with a Wheeled Cart

If your kitchen needs more horizontal surfaces for prep, storage, or just about anything, consider getting a wheeled cart. A small cart you can move around has so many uses! It can:

• Provide extra counter space.

• Function as a mini–kitchen island or bar cart.

• Offer a storage solution, particularly for items like nicer cookbooks that you might not want near spill-prone areas.

• Be a stand for plants, adding some green to your space or some fresh herbs to your cooking.

   If your cart outlives its usefulness in the kitchen, you can always roll it along to the bathroom, laundry room, or another spot where you might need it in the future.

5 Kitchen Cleaning Tools & Supplies You Really Need

Whether you're setting up a new kitchen, attempting to fit things into a tiny space, or trying to be more minimalist in your habits, it's good to know that you don't need a million products to clean your kitchen. Here's what you do need:

1. All-purpose cleaner, whether store-bought or DIY: This will work for most countertops and the inside of your fridge. Consider also getting a disinfectant spray to kill any germs that regular soap didn't catch. To make your own cleaner, simply mix 1 cup of water with ½ cup of white vinegar in a spray bottle. Slowly add 2 tablespoons of baking soda and shake gently.

2. Dish and hand soap: You know, for cleaning.

3. A broom: And ideally a dustpan, though you can use a stiff piece of paper or cardboard too.

4. A wet/dry mop for cleaning the floor and dusting: Buy the accompanying wet/dry cloths or just use rags, either soaked in cleaner or dry, depending on the task.

5. Sponges: Look for the type with one soft and one scrubbing side, for washing dishes and cleaning countertops and other surfaces.

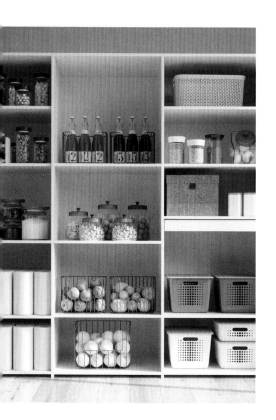

Discover the Joy of Baskets, Bins, and Trays

Sometimes, especially in urban apartments, you're stuck with a kitchen that lacks adequate cabinet space or is otherwise just not easy to organize. One solution: Group items together in a catchall.

It's partly a trick of the eye; visually, a random collection of olive oil bottles standing on your countertop looks messy, but if you arrange those same bottles on a pretty tray on that countertop, suddenly it looks intentional. Paper towel rolls on top of the fridge makes your kitchen look like a utility closet, but stick them in a large wicker basket and it looks organized and visually pleasing. This method also makes cleaning easier: Instead of ten olive oil bottles, you have to move only one tray to wipe the counter.

Beautify Your Food Storage

Remove nonperishable foods like cereal, pasta, and flour from their packaging and store them in jars or bins of the same size and shape. This will keep them fresher longer, make them less vulnerable to vermin, and help create an attractive, space-saving storage area.

Use Storage Products Thoughtfully

Storage containers can occasionally be the solution to a kitchen conundrum. But they also run the risk of becoming space-hogging clutter themselves. When organizing your kitchen, don't rush to buy specialized containers until you've carefully considered whether you need them—and measured to be sure they'll fit where you want them.

Make Life Easier with Labels

Labels can be game-changing in the kitchen, and they're more versatile than you might imagine. Here are just a few possibilities:

- In the fridge and freezer, label home-cooked and frozen foods to remind yourself what's what and when it was made. Divide a fridge with roommates by adding labels to shelves or plastic storage bins.

- In cabinets and on shelves, label storage bins, baskets, and boxes. Reduce cooking confusion by labeling jars of similar-looking ingredients, like wheat pasta and rice pasta.

- Under the sink, label containers of homemade cleansers and the top of spray bottles (so you can see what they are while looking down at them).

There's almost no limit to what you can label, whether you use a label maker, gift tags and ribbons, or plain old tape and markers.

CHAPTER

2

Dining Room

Eat, Drink, and Be Organized

A dining room can be different things to different people: It might be a *formal* room reserved for dinners with guests, or a *casual* room where your family grabs a quick bite in the morning. To help you achieve that goal, this chapter is packed with dozens of cleaning tips and organizational ideas to make your chores easier and give you more time to focus on what matters: food, drink, and company in a room you love.

5 Things to Declutter in Your Dining Room

Certain items always seem to end up in the dining room, even though they don't belong there. If you need to sort out your dining room, a good first step is to check for—and remove—the usual suspects:

1. Outerwear: Unless your dining room is home to a coat rack or hooks intended specifically for this purpose, your jackets and scarves do not need to be here.

2. Shoes: Like coats, shoes tend to congregate near where you enter your home. If they're in the dining room, return them to wherever they should go.

3. Bags: You say you'll just drop your bag on the table for a minute, and two weeks later it's still there. Time to put it away, plus any bag friends it may have made!

4. Mail, including packages: Open and sort through letters and boxes, deal with them, and do all the necessary filing, shredding, and recycling in one step rather than letting everything pile up on the table.

5. Forgotten objects from other rooms: Whether it's a mug from the kitchen or the TV remote from the living room, take a minute to return it to its home.

Get to the Root of Your Clutter

It's easy to say, and easy to do *in theory*: Just take the dirty dishes off the table and put the coats back in the closet. But in real life, sometimes we don't notice clutter until it's out of control.

So how do you prevent the mess in the first place? Look for patterns: Ask yourself what kind of stuff sneaks in, and why? For example, if shoes pile up in the dining room, maybe there's no obvious place to put them. Set up a shoe tray in the entryway, and the footwear should stay put. Or, if your love of knickknacks is making your dining room look like a gift shop, set aside one small area especially for tchotchkes and say goodbye to any that don't fit. In the future, make a "one in, one out" rule: Now you can buy a new toy only if you get rid of another.

Embrace Minimalism in the Dining Room

If you don't want to spend a lot of time cleaning the dining room or organizing its contents, adopt a minimalist approach in that space. Here's how:

• Declutter. Sell or give away everything you don't actually need.

• Center the room around one piece, like a huge dining table, an unusual paint color, or an overhead light that makes a statement. Focusing on a single, attention-getting element means you need less in the way of decor to create a visually interesting room.

• Choose furniture and objects that are simple and streamlined, like a sleek midcentury console. These have fewer surfaces to gather dust and are easier to clean. An ornate antique buffet, on the other hand, probably has a lot of crevices that will need cleaning.

Assemble a Cozy Coffee & Tea Station

If your vibe is less chardonnay and more chamomile, you can forgo a bar cart and make a corner of your dining room into a dreamy little tea and coffee spot.

Simply gather an accordion hanger and hardware to hang it, desk organizers for small or medium-sized items, and containers for sugar and whatever else you use in your tea or coffee. Place the drink-making items on a console table large enough to hold everything you need to make your drink (be sure to have an outlet nearby if you are using a small appliance).

Next, attach your accordion hanger to the wall at a height you can easily reach that's well above the top of your table. Hang mugs from their handles from the pegs on the accordion hanger.

If it works with your dining room layout and style, add a comfy chair, plant, or other touches to create a cozy nook.

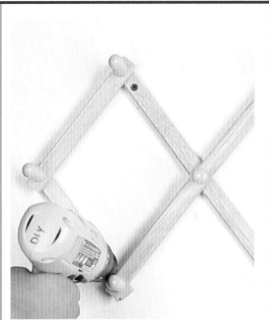

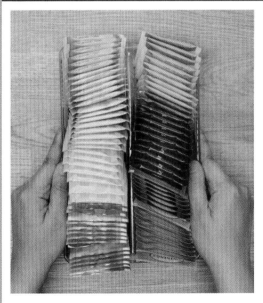

Clean These Out-of-the-Way Items

Every room has those little areas that are easily neglected, and the dining room is no exception. Here are some easy-to-miss spots to watch for when you're cleaning:

- **Under the table:** That's right, *all* the way under. Dust and crumbs can really travel, so when you're vacuuming around the chairs, make sure you also reach under the table.

- **Light fixtures:** Look closely. Is that glass globe looking a little murky? You might have forgotten to clean it for the past year or so. Also: ceiling fans.

- **Curtains and blinds:** Clean these regularly so they don't end up in a scary state.

- **Chair cushions and upholstery:** Even if they don't seem like they're getting dirty, dust accumulates over time. Vacuum them; then plump the cushions to freshen them up.

- **Baseboards:** They sit quietly where the wall meets the floor, attracting no notice until they're suddenly covered in dust. Run a sponge or microfiber cloth over them every once in a while to prevent dust buildup.

- **Placemats:** If they're being used, they're probably getting dirty. Wash or wipe them frequently or even after each use.

Protect Your Dining Room Table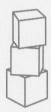

Your dining room table is likely one of your best pieces of furniture, which means you want to take care of it. If you're not already doing these simple things to safeguard your table, start now:

- **Put coasters under drinks and placemats under plates.** Don't forget to put one under your centerpieces!

- **Place trivets under serving dishes** to protect your table and sideboard from heat.

- **Use a tablecloth.** Placemats and trivets can protect certain spots, but a tablecloth provides more coverage.

- **Kid-proof your table the way restaurants do:** Cover it with paper. Add some crayons and you've got furniture protection and entertainment in one!

Don't Fall Into the Catchall Trap

In many homes, the dining room's proximity to the front door makes it a dumping ground for coats, bags, keys, packages—you name it. Designate a proper home for those things so they don't crowd your dining room with clutter.

Be Realistic

Social media pics of luxurious dining rooms can influence you to buy a bunch of stuff you won't actually use (but you *will* have to clean) or make you feel like you should turn your casual space into a formal one. Those pictures might not represent what's happening in your day-to-day life, though. Design your dining room around your *real* life and how you use the space, and it will be much easier to maintain.

Do a Clean (Table) Sweep

Don't let dishes linger on your dining table. Make it a dining room (or kitchen!) policy that after every meal or snack, plates and cups get put in the dishwasher or washed and returned to their cabinets.

Limit the Decor

You don't have to add a boatload of decor items if what you actually use in the dining room is pretty as well as practical. Nice plates, table linens, or candles can be all the display you need. These items are functional and can add a ton of visual interest. You can also add some natural seasonal decor, like spring and summer flowers, autumn leaves, or winter pine cones or holly berries as unique and beautiful centerpieces. And you can just toss them into your compost or yard waste bags when it's time to replace them.

Use a Mirror to Make Your Dining Room Feel Bigger

To make a small dining room feel larger, hang a circular mirror on the wall. The mirror can reflect natural light or light from a chandelier to brighten the space as well.

Find Creative Dining Room Storage Spots

If you need help thinking of unique storage ideas for a small dining room, here are some additional ways to stretch your space. These ideas are useful *and* look amazing:

- Install a crown molding shelf all along your walls, about three-quarters of the way up. Gallery walls can be incredibly hard to pull off, so use this narrow shelf as a way to display framed pictures, plates, or other artwork to get a similar effect.

- Find a small corner shelf to take advantage of an otherwise unusable triangle of space.

- Hang plates directly on walls. A gallery wall of dinnerware can be eye-catching if you arrange it properly, and it also saves you storage space. Just be very careful when installing hardware, and maybe save this option for plates you wouldn't be devastated to lose if they fell down.

Don't Let Dust Accumulate

If you don't use your dining room often, you might think you can go weeks without cleaning it. But unfortunately, that's not how life—or dust—works. Give the room a regular dusting every two weeks to prevent the dust bunnies from taking over.

Try Microfiber Cloths

To avoid using a million paper towels every time you dust, invest in reusable microfiber cloths. Use them to dust, then toss them in the washer so they'll be ready for the next time.

Dust Drapes with Your Vacuum

While you're cleaning the dining room floor, make sure you get the drapes too. It's not equivalent to a deep-cleaning, but you can regularly dust window treatments with the soft brush attachment of a vacuum.

Make Your Own Glass Cleaner

To keep the windows and mirrors in your dining room sparkling while saving money on store-bought cleaners, make an easy DIY glass cleaner by stirring a few drops of dishwashing liquid into 2 cups of warm water. Or fill a spray bottle with a mixture of 1 cup of water, 1 cup of rubbing alcohol, and 1 tablespoon of white vinegar.

Make Your Own *Bar Cart* from Two End Tables

WHAT YOU NEED:

- 2 small tables of the same size
- Paint and paintbrush, or contact paper, ruler, and needle or small sharp knife (optional)
- Towel rack and screws
- Drill and drill bits
- 4 corner brackets and screws
- 4 wheels and screws (optional)

For such a simple piece of furniture, bar carts are usually super expensive. But if you have some old end tables or nightstands you don't use, you can make your own!

HOW TO DO IT:

1. If you want to change the look of your tables, paint them or cover them with contact paper. If you use contact paper, carefully smooth down the paper on the tables (a ruler can help you do this) and use a needle or small knife to pop any air bubbles.

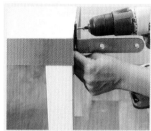

2. Attach the towel rack to the side of one table (this table will be the top half of your bar cart).

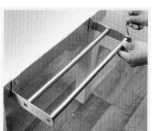

3. Stack the top table onto the bottom table, then secure them by drilling corner brackets to the inside of each of the top table legs and the surface of the lower table.

4. Optional: If you want wheels, turn your bar cart upside down and use your drill to attach wheels to each of the bottom legs.

5. Arrange drinks, glasses, and anything else you want on your new bar cart!

5 Hacks for Reviving Old Wood Floors

If a damaged wood floor is making your dining room look dull, try these tips for making old floors feel new again:

1. To minimize scratches, mix equal parts white vinegar and olive oil in a spray bottle. Spray onto the scratch and rub with a cloth to smooth over.

2. To darken areas that are too light, put a few black tea bags in a mug of boiling water. Let steep (the longer it sits, the darker the stain). Rub the tea onto the discoloration with a cloth. Repeat as needed.

3. To reduce scuff marks on unpolished floors, gently buff away scuff marks with a Magic Eraser.

4. To smooth over dents, cover the dent with a cloth. Press and rub an iron over the cloth, using steam, for a few minutes. The dent should swell until smooth or nearly smooth.

5. To eliminate creaky boards, shake baby powder between the affected boards. Use a paintbrush to brush the powder into the crack.

Protect Your Wood Floor

Keep your dining room's wood floor looking good by putting protective gliders on your dining chairs (and any other pieces of furniture that you slide around a lot). These can be nylon discs that you nail on, or felt stickers that you peel and place on the bottom of your chair legs.

Remove Common Stains from Your Dining Room Carpet

Spills are bound to happen eventually when you put a rug under a table. Don't panic, though: Some seemingly terrible stains are actually easy to remove with products you already have in your home.

- **Red wine:** Use a towel to dab at the wine to soak up as much as possible. Douse the stain in white vinegar, letting it sit for at least 15 minutes. Blot (don't rub!) to get rid of any vinegar that hasn't soaked in. Sprinkle with baking soda and brush at the stain with a wet toothbrush. Rinse the baking soda with water.

- **Chocolate:** Let harden and scrape off the excess with a butter knife. Mix ¼ teaspoon of liquid laundry detergent into 1 cup of water and pour the mixture over the stain, letting it sit for a few minutes. Gently scrub the stain with a toothbrush and blot off the excess with a towel. Rinse with water.

- **Coffee:** Soak up any excess coffee with a towel, then drench the remaining stain in a mixture of a few drops of liquid laundry detergent in 1 cup of water. Carefully blot the stain until you see most of the coffee soaking up into the towel. Soak the remaining stain in a little vinegar and blot. Repeat these steps until the stain is completely gone. Rinse with water.

- **Candle wax:** Cover the stain with a damp towel and iron for about 30 seconds with medium-high heat. Transfer out the towel once it's covered with wax. (Be sure not to iron the carpet directly!) Soak the remaining stain in rubbing alcohol for a few minutes and scrub with a toothbrush. Rinse with water.

Save a Scratched Serving Platter

Light-colored platters and plates show small scrapes and scratches easily. To remove the marks, wet your platter, sprinkle on a small amount of powdered scouring cleanser, and gently scrub away scuffs with a damp scrubber. Then simply wash with soap and water.

Take Care of Your China and Silver

Whether you inherited a family heirloom or love thrifting for mismatched gems, you can end up with a lovely set of dinnerware that you have no idea how to clean. Here are some tips to maintain vintage pieces:

- Wash by hand in warm water using mild detergent. (If your pieces are dishwasher-safe, load them far apart to prevent chipping.) Avoid using bleach and cleaning near metal utensils that can cause scratches.

- For lightly stained china dinnerware, try a baking soda and water paste or a salt and white vinegar scrub. Remove tea stains from cups by soaking in warm water with a denture tablet.

- For serious stains on china, soak pieces in a tub with 1 tablespoon each of baking soda and white vinegar for every 1 cup of warm water. Or soak in 20 percent hydrogen peroxide, then hand-wash. Test first in an inconspicuous spot to avoid damaging delicate items.

- No matter what cleaning method you use, always be extra careful with gold-rimmed pieces. They can be damaged by harsh or abrasive cleansers or scrub brushes.

- If your china is *crazed* (that doesn't mean your dishes have gone wild; it's the term for small cracks in the glaze), it is no longer food-safe and shouldn't be used to serve food.

- To brighten up dull silver pieces on display in your dining room, line a pot with aluminum foil. Add 1 cup each of baking soda and salt and pour in enough boiling water to cover the items. Then let the silver pieces soak for up to 30 minutes before polishing.

5 Ways to Carve Out a Dining Room When It's Not Its Own Room

Here are some tricks for mentally and visually dividing one space from the other—and making the whole thing look neat:

1. Arrange a long, low row of storage cubes that are open on both sides. This splits a larger space in half without cutting it off entirely, and gives you a new storage area.

2. Use a folding screen. A folding screen visually blocks off one part of a room from another, allowing you to conceal a bed in a studio apartment or hide a home office when you don't want to think about work.

3. Place large plants between two sections of a space to form a natural barrier. They'll add life and color to your home while doing double duty as a room divider.

4. Use a couch as a wall. If your dining room and living room are one space, position the living room couch with its back to the dining area to separate the two sections.

5. Paint the room two colors. This option takes up zero space and can have a big impact. Using paint can subtly—or boldly!—separate two areas.

Size Your Dining Room Rug Properly

A rug that's too large or too small can make a dining room look cramped or sloppy. Here's a simple formula to ensure yours is sized right: Measure your dining room table and find a rug that extends at least two feet beyond it on all four sides.

For a different twist on the traditional rug look, go for round or oval instead of rectangular to create visual contrast with your table.

Be the Judge: Chairs versus Bench

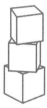

Though chairs are still the norm, a bench can be a great choice in a dining room. How do these two options stack up in terms of cleaning and organizing? Here are some pros of each:

• Chairs are easier to move around for flexible seating arrangements—and for cleaning the floor.

• Benches and chairs can both provide extra storage space under the seat, but benches, being larger, can definitely store more.

• Benches can help pack more people into a smaller space, especially if kids are involved.

• Depending on the room's layout, a bench can be tucked against a wall or under the table to save space.

Of course, there's always a third option: a mix of both!

3

Living Room

A Place for Everything (When Everything's in Its Place)

Living rooms are where we **relax**, hang out, and entertain. From quiet Sundays bingeing way too much TV to raucous game nights, the living room is where the **fun** happens. Because we use our living rooms for so many things, there's usually a lot of stuff there—blankets and magazines and toys...and is that yesterday's coffee mug? Making a simple organization and storage plan for this room will mean you spend less time on chores and more time relaxing there!

Prioritize Getting Comfy

Your living room is all about comfort and coziness, so remember as you set out to clean and organize that it shouldn't be a space you're scared to use! Forgo light-colored fabrics that won't clean up easily, breakable decor, and uncomfortable furniture and instead look for easy-to-maintain, livable items.

Hide an Electronic Eyesore

Necessities like thermostats, intercoms, and power panels aren't clutter, but they can stick out like a sore thumb and ruin the organized look of an otherwise beautiful room. To artfully hide those annoying boxes on your walls, paint or otherwise decorate a shallow wooden box or a framed canvas from an art supply store. Attach two hinges to one side of the back of the box or canvas. Screw the hinges to the wall next to the thermostat or panel so that the artwork can flap open to reveal the electronic eyesore and flap shut to hide it.

Don't Let Stray Items Stay

Living rooms are handy hiding places for things that belong in other rooms. Do a regular sweep for sweaters, mugs, shoes, toys, and other things that don't permanently live in the living room and return them to their homes.

Don't Confuse "Homey" with "Messy"

Blankets, rugs, throw pillows, extra seating, and all those cozy things make a living room awesome. But you can go too far with accessories. If your living room looks like the aftermath of a Black Friday sale in the home accessories department of a big-box store, it's time to scale it back.

Modernize the Room

Often, the most dated living room features—think pleated lampshades, bulky recliners, or elaborate window treatments—are also the items that make the room harder to keep neat and clean. If you don't absolutely love them, try exchanging them for more modern alternatives.

Get Rid of One Big Thing

A quick hack for a more livable living room is to remove one large item—usually a piece of furniture—that you just never use. You may have gotten used to looking at that tired, saggy armchair no one sits in anymore, but you won't miss it for a minute when it's gone!

Get Rid of Pet Hair in Seconds Flat

If you have a cat or dog, you know the fur struggle is real. Here's a simple way to get pet hair off couch cushions, upholstered chairs, or curtains: Put on a rubber glove! Then just run your hand over the area. The static created by the friction between the rubber and the fabric will wipe away fur in seconds.

Work Your Pets' Gear Into Your Decor

In addition to the obvious dog beds and cat trees, there are plenty of other ways to make pet items part of your space without letting their stuff take over:

• Organized humans' love of vertical space is shared by cats, who feel comfortable up high above the action. Install a series of narrow shelves a few feet below the ceiling so they can roam in their own zone.

• For chilled-out kitties, hang a shelf just below a window to give them their own viewing platform.

• If your dog loves their crate and also loves hanging out where you are, semi-conceal the crate inside or under a piece of stylish furniture (or spring for a high-end dog crate that doubles as furniture). For example, you could tuck the crate under a unique end table.

- For pets who live in a cage, customize or source one that looks less utilitarian and more like a part of your decor.

- A fish tank can be a fascinating and relaxing focal point of the room.

Get a New Look Without Getting New Stuff

If your living room desperately needs a new look but the last thing you need is more things to tidy, make a change that will revive your space without cluttering it. Here are some ways to make it happen:

- **Change your paint color or add wallpaper.** Remember you can paint brick and tile too, so a boring fireplace is a good candidate for a makeover even if you don't want to deal with the entire room.

- **Hang up a mirror.** Mirrors make any space look bigger and come in so many styles that they can convey pretty much any vibe you like.

- **Add, change, or remove rugs.** (Or the advanced level of this option: Change your flooring.)

- **Update your upholstery in minor ways.** Switch your pillow covers or slip-cover, or add new cushion covers to chairs.

- **Swap in new doorknobs or drawer pulls.** It's a subtle change, but can make a room more fun, more grown-up, more colorful—more anything!

- **Install a ceiling rose for lighting, crown molding around the ceiling perimeter, or beadboard on the walls.** These decorative changes don't take up any space, but they make a big impact and can seriously alter the look of a room.

- **Add or remove a door.** If your living room is already closed off, removing the door can improve the flow with the rest of the house; on the flip side, if there's no door, adding one (if possible) can create a more private and cozy space.

Clean This Gross Stuff in the Living Room Right Now

You vacuum the floor and wipe down the coffee table, but other areas and objects in the living room are also magnets for dust, dirt, and germs. If you want to get your living room really clean, make sure to tackle these tasks too:

- Disinfect remote controls, light switches, doorknobs, thermostats, and any other frequent touch points.
- Clean any piece of furniture your pets like to sit on, sleep on, or chew on.
- Dust inside the fireplace, where cobwebs can linger unnoticed.
- Wash throws, area rugs, and curtains.
- Clean up the areas around and under your plants, where soil, water droplets, and fallen leaves can lurk.
- Dust electronics and cables.

Clean Up after Your Candles

If your festive candles left a memory you don't want, wait for the wax to fully harden, then carefully chip off drips with an old credit card or razor blade. Wipe away soot streaks with a Magic Eraser.

Get Rid of Greasy Spots on Walls with Chalk

If little ones have left greasy little handprints on your painted living room walls, here's a surprising item that can remove them: chalk. Rub a piece of chalk over the smudges and wait for 10 minutes. Wipe first with a dry microfiber cloth, then again with a damp one.

Erase Scuffs from Leather Furniture

Rub shoe wax polish on your leather couches and chairs to smooth over scuffs and scratches. First make sure the color matches by testing it in an inconspicuous spot. Apply a small amount to clean leather, wait, then buff off completely with a cloth.

4 Ways to Pare Down Your Collections

Whether they're sentimental, they're worth a lot of money, they're conversation pieces, or they're representative of your past, it's not easy to get rid of collections you've been accumulating for years or even decades. Here's how to finally pass on or pare down the collectibles in your living room:

1. Choose a few special pieces. Pick a handful of your favorites and let the rest go.

2. Think about who you are now. If the collection dates from your childhood or teen years, you might be a totally different person now (say, a person who doesn't need fifty-eight porcelain frog figurines).

3. Think about selling. If your main regret is spending money on all this stuff, try to let that thought go. You enjoyed these things, after all! And if they're still worth a lot, you may be able to sell them.

4. Celebrate new technology. You might be able to convert bulky boxes of VHS tapes, childhood photos, or typewritten papers into digital versions that preserve their content while taking up space only in the cloud.

Get Rid of Items You Don't Need

With all the little items that end up in your living room, there's bound to be a boxful (at least) of things you'll be happy to part with. Here are some things to look for when you're doing a living room purge:

- **Old pillows and throws:** Are they still in good shape? Do you really use them all? Do they fit with the overall look and feel of the room? If not, let them go.

- **Furniture you don't use:** Maybe you initially thought you needed two side tables, or a floor lamp, but now you never use them.

- **Decor you feel meh about:** If you don't need or love these accessories, go ahead and get rid of them.

- **Old magazines:** Flip through your stack and recycle the ones you'll never look at again.

Learn to Part with Books

For many people, books are one of the hardest belongings to part with. Here's how to streamline your library:

- **Define why you keep books.** Maybe you really want only those books you'll definitely reread, or you want to keep your all-time favorites, or the ones that hold certain memories of times in your life. Once you decide which books are most important, some of the titles currently on your shelves will no longer seem worth keeping.

- **Consider an e-reader.** It's not for everyone, but if you like reading on a device and some of your books don't need to be, well, books, you can replace the paper titles with their virtual counterparts.

- **Make a list of your favorites.** If you're primarily holding on to unread books so you won't forget about them, write a list of all your books before letting some go. If you ever really need one of those books again, you can always find another copy.

- **Cut out a category.** Maybe there's a group of books you can get rid of, such as college textbooks.

- **Drop the duplicates.** Unless you specifically collect different translations of the *Odyssey*, you probably don't need multiple copies of the same book. Pick one and say goodbye to the others.

Find Space Behind the Sofa

In place of a coffee table or end table—or in addition to them—take advantage of that skinny space behind your couch and put a slim table there. Often overlooked as dead space, it can be a convenient spot for glasses, remotes, and other small objects. You can get as decorative or practical as you want with your skinny table—for example, if there's an outlet back there, try going practical and put a charging station for your phone there. If you can't find a table that fits the bill, it's easy enough to make your own with a slim board, some legs (and hardware to attach them), and a can of paint or stain.

Think Beyond Bookshelves

If you have a lot of books, there are many ways to organize and display them beyond the classic built-in bookshelves or bookcases. Try some of these alternatives:

- Stack large and rarely read books so they become artsy side tables.
- Lay books on their sides, spines facing out, and simply stack them up against the wall for a casual bohemian look.
- Make a coffee table out of four or six storage cubes and fill it with books.
- Keep kids' books on a rolling cart, like their own little roving library.

5 Amazing Uses for Baskets and Bins

These all-purpose, whole-house solutions are especially welcome in the living room, where there are so many things they can hold. Here are some suggestions for the endless ways they can help you stay organized:

1. Place a large woven basket beside the couch and fill it with extra blankets and pillows.

2. Label bins with your kids' names, and have them put their toys inside when playtime is done.

3. Put laptops, phones, and other devices into a rectangular woven basket to transition WFH time to screen-free time.

4. Keep extra batteries, plugs, cables, and other electronic odds and ends in a discreet bin in or near the media console.

5. Keep sewing or knitting projects and supplies in a basket by your favorite chair so you can work on them when you want and stash them away when you need to.

Get Creative with Furniture

Because the living room is usually more relaxed and less formal than, say, the dining room, you can feel free to use nontraditional furniture or totally unexpected pieces for storage. Imagine a vintage metal file cabinet as a coffee table or an old card catalog as a console.

Look for Living Room Furniture That Does Double Duty

In a small living room, you can have furniture or storage space, but not both. Just kidding—you can totally have both! In fact, some of the swankiest living room furniture doubles as extra storage. Here are some ways to do it:

- Use a blanket chest, chest of drawers, or vintage trunk for a coffee table. It adds a lot of individuality to the room, and it opens up to hold a bunch of blankets and pillows. (This tip is especially helpful if your couch is also a guest bed.)

- Choose an ottoman that opens. These already versatile pieces of furniture become even more handy when they're made with a top that lifts off, revealing a storage compartment beneath. Some ottoman tops also flip to function as a tray!

- Buy or make side tables or end tables with drawers.

- Use storage cubes, wooden crates, or vintage suitcase stacks as tables.

Assemble a *Side Table* with Sly Storage

WHAT YOU NEED:

- Stain and paintbrush
- Circular piece of wood (diameter should be larger than the cake pan diameter)
- 3 long screw-on table legs with brackets
- Round metal cake pan
- Drill and drill bits
- Cutting pliers
- Hot glue gun
- Spray paint

Out of all the rooms in your house, the living room is perhaps the easiest in which to add all kinds of stealthy storage areas. Case in point: this li'l side table with a secret hidey-hole.

HOW TO DO IT:

1. Stain the circular tabletop and legs.

2. Screw the leg brackets onto the bottom of the cake pan in a triangle shape. Use the pliers to snip the ends of the screws (the part that sticks out the other side), then cover over each with a dab of hot glue.

3. When hardened, paint with spray paint and let dry.

4. Screw the table legs into the brackets and stand the table base upright.

5. Place the wooden circle on top. Now you can display a potted plant or other decorative item on top of your side table, while safely stashing eyeglasses and other small items beneath in the hidden compartment that no one will guess started out in the baking aisle!

Create Activity Zones

This organizing tactic works wonders in any room where lots of different things happen. And the living room, with its lounging, game-playing, TV-watching, and so on, is the perfect example.

To make tidying easier and to bring some visual order to a large living room, designate different sections of the space. Stack board games in a nook with a small table and two comfy chairs; create a children's area with a brightly colored rug beside a cubby stocked with toys; and separate a sanctuary for readers by placing a loveseat, a tiny tea table, and an adjustable floor lamp beside the bookcase.

Make Your Living Room Kid-Friendly

If your kids—or someone else's—spend a lot of time in your living room, these simple tips can make organizing and cleaning easier:

- Cover a corner of the floor with a soft area rug or two. It's more comfortable to sit on, and it helps define this spot as their own space.

- Choose furniture in a material like acrylic that's easy to wipe down.

- Use a slipcover on your couch and covers on your throw pillows for easier cleaning.

- Store breakable items higher up or in a shelving unit with glass doors.

- If you have the space, put kid-sized furniture in or near a corner they can call "theirs." In a smaller living room, dedicate the lowest shelf on a bookcase to them while reserving higher storage areas for adults, and consider options like nesting coffee tables or end tables, where the lower piece can be pulled out temporarily.

4 Ways to Make the Most of Your Wall Space

Even the tiniest of living rooms usually have some overlooked wall space. Here are some ways to get more out of your walls:

1. Mount your TV and lighting. If there's no place for the footprint of a TV table or standing lamp, attach them to a wall. Wall sconces or pendant lights suspended from hooks can be great space-saving alternatives to lamps.

2. Hang photos and decorative items. It's good enough for museums, right? Arrange larger pieces higher up to really take advantage of unused space.

3. Choose hanging plants. Hang some trailing vines from the ceiling or high up on a wall to create a beautiful alternative to traditional potted greenery on tables or shelves.

4. Install floating shelves. These are a fave in organizing circles because they're just so versatile. You can put them at any height and in any arrangement, and they come in any length, from a few inches to many feet. That's a flexibility you just can't get from standing shelving units.

Reclaim an Unused Fireplace to Save Space

If your living room has a fireplace that's currently defunct, consider placing shelves in the empty space. You could attach two or three shelves stretching all the way across the inside of the fireplace, or simply place a shelving unit there.

Get Cozy Without the Clutter

Whether you call it cozy, hygge, or just staying in, you want your living room full of warm and inviting things during cold weather. But you don't want it *too* full. Here's how to get that sweater weather vibe without tripping over your stuff:

- **Adjust the lighting.** Go for soft light from bulbs or candles.

- **Go for throws.** A few warm blankets go a long way; stick to one color palette for a neater look.

- **Bring the outdoors in.** Decorating with found items like branches, pine cones, and leaves is calming and free—and you can easily declutter by returning them back into nature.

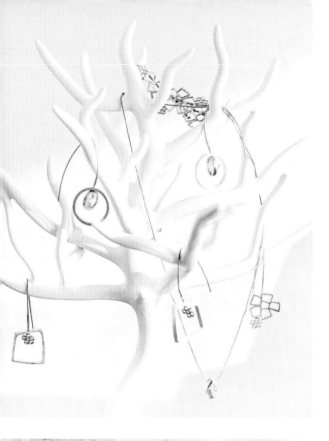

4

Bedroom

Put the Chaos to Bed

Your bedroom is your **sanctuary**, where you relax, recharge, and wake up **refreshed** and ready to start your day. This chapter is all about creating a bedroom that is practical and functional but also feels cozy and calm. Once you incorporate the ideas in this chapter, you'll spend a lot less time stressing and a lot more time *sleeping peacefully*.

Create Calm

The last thing you want when you're reading, sleeping, or getting dressed for the day is to feel uncomfortable or stressed out. That's why it's so important to cultivate a relaxing vibe in your bedroom. From your color scheme to your cleaning routine, the goal is to maintain your bedroom as a calming environment.

Ask Yourself What You (Really) Need in Your Bedroom

If you're trying to eliminate clutter from your bedroom, you might be wondering what really *is* necessary to keep there. Though the answer will be different for everyone, here's a good place to start thinking about essential bedroom elements:

- **A bed:** Or, to be more specific, something comfortable to sleep on, whether it's a traditional four-poster, a futon, a floor mattress, a daybed, or another option.

- **A nightstand or bedside table (or two):** This does not have to be a piece of furniture; you might prefer to use a tray to corral the items you keep by your bed.

- **A place to store clothing:** This can be a closet, a chest of drawers, a shelving unit, a clothes rail, storage bins, or some combination of these.

- **Lighting:** Your bedroom may already have a ceiling light that provides all the illumination you need; if not, add one or two lamps.

- **A mirror:** Unless you're checking your outfit in a full-length mirror elsewhere in the house, you'll probably want a bedroom mirror. This can slip over the back of the door without adding clutter.

Clean That Bedding

In case you were wondering, you should be washing your sheets every week or two, your blankets or comforter or duvet cover at least two or three times a year (it's easy to remember to do this when the seasons change), and your pillows every three to six months.

Clean Bedroom Carpets

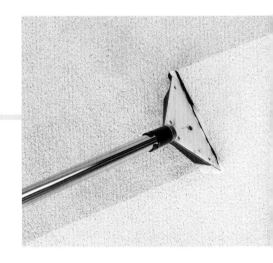

Bedroom carpets don't usually amass a lot of stains, unless you eat in there regularly. Still, they can eventually start to look tired or matted. To refresh your carpet, deep-clean it once a year. You can rent a carpet cleaner and wash it yourself, hire a pro to do the job, or purchase a steam cleaner if you have a lot of carpeting in your house.

Deodorize Your Mattress

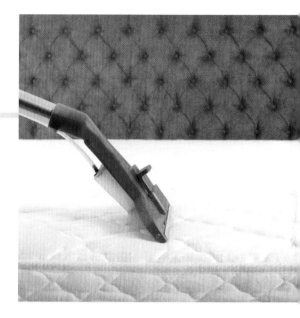

Mattresses accumulate dust and absorb smells, just like any other upholstered item. To get it smelling fresh, just sprinkle your mattress with baking soda (optional: mix in a few drops of essential oil for scent) and rub it in. Let it sit for 1 hour, then vacuum up the baking soda—along with all those dead skin cells and dust mites and other stuff you'd *really* rather not think about. If baking soda can't fully get rid of an odor, spray the mattress with a multipurpose household disinfectant. (Bonus mattress tip: Flip and rotate it every few months to help it wear more evenly.)

Corral Trash

If you don't already have one, put a small wastebasket in your bedroom. Choose a pretty color or cool style to make it blend in with your decor.

3 Common Stains You Can Get Out of a Mattress

Absorbent mattresses seem to gobble up any liquids spilled on them. Here's how to eliminate or at least minimize common mattress stains:

1. Food, drinks, or dirt: Many stains can be remedied with a simple mix of two parts hydrogen peroxide to one part dish soap. Use a scrub brush or old toothbrush to rub the mixture into the mattress, then wipe with a damp cloth.

2. Blood: Use a cloth to wet the spot with cold water. Dab or spray with hydrogen peroxide. Blot with a clean cloth and let dry.

3. Sweat or urine: Spray the affected areas with a mixture of 1 part dish soap, 2 parts hydrogen peroxide, and 1 teaspoon baking soda and let dry.

Some general tips to keep in mind:

• If you can, clean up spills immediately rather than letting them sit.

• Mattresses, especially memory-foam toppers, should not get wet if you can possibly avoid it. When using water or liquid cleansers, spray lightly or dab with a cloth rather than pouring.

• For tough stains, you might need to repeat these steps several times.

• To prevent future damage—and reduce your cleaning tasks—get a mattress protector.

Cut Cleaning Time with These Shortcuts

These quick, minimal-effort activities go a long way to cleaning up a bedroom:

- Can't wash or change your sheets right now? At least do the pillowcases. If you find yourself wanting to change or swap them regularly, buy extra pillowcases so you can have clean ones anytime you want.

- Clean your floor with a mop or wet cloth. It's less work than vacuuming or dusting, but it still wipes up a lot of icky stuff—and can disinfect too!

- Wipe down your windowsills.

- Dust the corners of the room, and around electronics and chair legs.

- Keep a paper shopping bag or cardboard box on hand to fill with items to donate. This tip gets some unwanted things out of the bedroom—and may motivate you to keep going till the box is full.

Try This Easiest Freshening Tip Ever

Want to make your bedroom feel fresh? Open the windows to air out the room.
That's it; that's the tip.

Rightsize Your Wardrobe

At its heart, decluttering comes down to asking yourself the right questions about the object you're looking at. Here's how to reduce your clothing collection so you keep only what you wear and love.

The physical process is easy. First, gather all your clothes into one place. (To make this more manageable, do only the current or upcoming season at a time.) Then, evaluate every item, sorting into four piles:

1. Keep. You love it, need it, and/or wear it often.

2. Throw out/use as rags. You don't want it, and no one else would either.

3. Donate/sell. You don't want it, but someone else might.

4. Fix. You'd totally wear it if that missing button is replaced.

The harder part is the decision itself. Ask yourself as you evaluate:

- Do I like this?

- Do I wear this?

- Does this fit my current body, lifestyle, activities, climate, and style?

- Am I hanging on to this for any reason other than that I like and wear it?

If you answer no to any of the first three questions, it's probably time to get rid of the item. If it's hard to make a decision, try these tips:

- **Be quick.** Trust your initial instinct.

- **Be honest.** If you don't already replace missing buttons or take clothes to the tailor, don't assume you'll start now.

- **Be positive.** Focus on the clothes that make you say "Oh, I love this!" and not the ones that make you say "Hmm, I don't know…"

- **Be relaxed.** If it stresses you out to discard clothes, put them in a box and wait six months. If you haven't thought about them, let alone retrieved them, let them go.

6 Steps to Organizing Your Closet Once and for All

If you want to organize your closet but have no idea where to start, follow these steps:

1. If your closet has shelves, separate what you're going to hang and what you're going to fold.

2. Whether you're hanging or folding clothes, start by sorting them by type—shirts together, jeans together, skirts together, pants together, and so on.

3. Within those categories, refine by style or function. For example, divide pants and tops into categories like office pants and casual pants, or short-sleeved, long-sleeved, and sleeveless tops.

4. Within that, refine further by color. The simplest method is to run through the rainbow or start with black and go from dark to light, ending with white clothes. Or use a different color system that you prefer.

5. Consider relocating a rarely worn category. If you only occasionally go to dressy events, set aside a small area of the closet, preferably at the back or at one end, and stow all the dressy clothes there.

6. Keep belts, ties, scarves, and other accessories together. If you're storing these in the closet, get an organizer that can keep them neat and accessible.

While you're organizing your closet, don't forget to clean it too. Vacuum the floor, dust the shelves, and do whatever else you'd do when cleaning any room.

Create More Space in a Small Closet

Here are some ways to maximize the square footage of your closet:

• In a small but deep closet, install a second rod behind the first to store double the clothes.

• Use the vertical space at the top of your closet. If there's no shelf, install one; if there's one shelf, maybe you can fit another above it.

• Use the space at the bottom of your closet. Place suitcases or storage bins here to store off-season or infrequently worn items.

• Put hooks or hanging storage bags over the door to make room for jackets, scarves, shoes, and more.

• Extend your closet into the room with a clothes rack. Do it right, and it can also serve as decoration or wardrobe inspiration—plus help you organize your current favorite items and keep them readily available.

Handle Your Hangers

Believe it or not, how you choose and use hangers can make organizing your closet easier.

• **Buy matching hangers.** Even if you don't care a bit about the way they look, choosing hangers that are uniform in size, shape, and color will help you store your clothes neatly so you can see what you really have.

• **Look for decent-quality hangers without sharp edges.** (Those wire things from the dry cleaner? Nooooo.)

• **Use hangers to see what you actually wear.** Try this tip: Turn all your hangers to face the opposite direction, then switch the hanger to the correct direction when you rehang the item after you've worn it. Switching the direction your hangers hang makes it clear what's getting worn and what isn't. If the entire winter goes by and you see that you never wore that one cardigan, consider ditching it.

Upcycle
a Boring File Cabinet Into a Unique Nightstand

WHAT YOU NEED:

- Metal filing cabinet with 2 drawers
- Washcloth
- Painter's tape
- Chalk paint
- Foam roller and paintbrush
- 2 (8 × 10-inch) picture frames
- Drill and drill bits
- 2 drawer pulls
- Epoxy
- Clear wax
- Soft-bristled brush

If you're looking for a nightstand that holds a lot of stuff (like your big stack of TBR books), one option is to make your own by upcycling an old filing cabinet.

HOW TO DO IT:

1. Remove the original drawer pulls from the cabinet drawers.

2. Wipe any dust or dirt off the file cabinet with a damp washcloth. Place painter's tape over any areas you don't want to get paint on.

3. Paint the cabinet and drawer fronts with chalk paint, using the foam roller.

4. Remove the back and the glass from the picture frames. Paint the frames the same color.

5. Drill pilot holes as necessary for the hardware of new drawer pulls, then attach them.

6. Place the picture frames so they're centered, one on the front of each drawer. Attach with epoxy.

7. Brush on a coat of clear wax to seal the paint all over the cabinet.

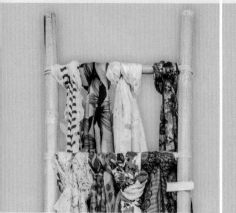

4 Ways to Get Ahold of Unruly Accessories

Once you've got your clothes sorted out, there's still the issue of all those other things you wear: scarves, hats, belts, bags...the list goes on and on. Here are some tips for dealing with accessories:

1. Hook circular shower curtain rings around a closet rod to hang bags by their handles. They take up very little space, and because they pop open and closed, your bags can't fall to the floor.

2. Use a decorative ladder as storage for scarves and shawls—and to complement your decor! (A ladder also looks lovely draped with extra blankets.)

3. Hang belts on a rack in your closet. Because belts have such a specific shape, they're one of the few items that benefit from a special organizing product. But all racks are not created equal: Look for the smallest one you can find to avoid taking up unnecessary closet space. (The same goes for ties.) If you own only one or two belts, a nail or hook inside the closet is all you need.

4. Hang hats instead of pictures. If you wear a lot of hats, create a hat gallery wall to show them off rather than let them fill up half your closet.

Look Through Your Accessories Collection

Even if you declutter your clothes fairly regularly, it's easy to let accessories accumulate unchecked. That's partly because they take up relatively little room and partly because unlike pants, you'll never stop fitting into a scarf!

To decide which to keep and which to let go of, ask yourself the same questions you would about a jacket or a pair of jeans. (Do I like this? Do I wear this? Does this fit my current body, lifestyle, activities, climate, and style? Am I hanging on to this for any reason other than that I like and wear it?) Donate, sell, or trash anything that doesn't make the cut.

Organize Your Jewelry

Jewelry boxes look sweet, but they're not strictly necessary. Instead, try incorporating your jewelry collection into your bedroom decor. Doubling practicality with style, this strategy puts items out in the open for easy access.

For example, earrings can be stored in mismatched teacups and saucers, vintage tins, or small wooden boxes. Rings can be displayed on a ring holder, bracelets draped on jewelry trees, and necklaces hung from pushpins on a corkboard.

If highly visible options aren't your style, go the opposite route with no-fuss jewelry storage like those sturdy, compartmentalized plastic boxes meant for screws and nails. These are also easy to grab if you travel or move, and can be stashed away in seconds.

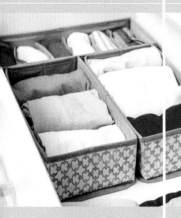

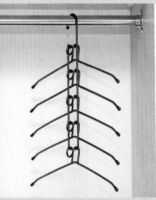

6 *Storage Products for Easy Bedroom Organization*

Some specialized organizing products don't always fit where they're supposed to, and they run the risk of becoming clutter themselves. But in a bedroom, there are a few general products that can really help sort out your stuff, especially if you're naturally messy or live in a small space:

1. Collapsible box organizers: Usually made of durable fabric, they fit all sorts of tricky items from socks to stationery to beauty products. Also, they take up almost no space folded up when not in use.

2. Layered or tiered hangers: These go by many names and come in various styles, all of which let you hang multiple items on one hanger.

3. Honeycomb or grid drawer dividers: Their structure keeps socks and under-wear from reverting to a jumbled mess in your drawer.

4. Shoe racks: They accommodate double or triple the number of shoes than would fit on the floor, and they can also serve as bookshelves or display shelves for keep-sakes or plants.

5. Vacuum storage bags: Get ready to magically make your off-season sweaters and blankets take up way less room in your closet.

6. Hanging jewelry organizers: They're handy if you have lots of jewelry and little storage space, especially if you also travel with your jewelry frequently. Keep pieces safely separated in individual pouches, hang the organizer in your closet for out-of-sight storage, and roll it all up to stash in a suitcase.

Store Your Off-Season Clothes

If there are seasons where you live and you're not putting away your off-season clothes, you might want to start. Here's why:

- When everything in your closet is something you can realistically wear *now*, getting dressed gets a lot quicker. Why waste time scanning the sweaters if it's T-shirt weather?

- Especially in small spaces, it makes closet organization easier and more pleasant.

- If you feel like your closet is packed but you have nothing to wear, seasonal storage gives you a more accurate picture. You might find that most of your clothes are for warmer weather, and you really do have nothing to wear when it's cold!

- It helps you declutter or downsize your wardrobe over the longer term. When you pull out that box of fall clothes you haven't seen in a year, it's easier to evaluate them with fresh eyes.

- If you live in a seasonless paradise, you still might consider rotating your clothes once or twice a year anyway, simply to save space or help with decluttering decisions.

Store Clothes Where You Put Them On

The bedroom is the natural place to store your clothes, but some pieces are outliers: Where do jackets go? Or shoes? How about winter coats and rain hats?

In general, it's easiest to organize your clothes (and to get dressed) if you store your clothes where you put them on. For most people, this means that clothes worn indoors (shirts, pants, skirts, intimates, loungewear) belong in the bedroom, and clothes reserved for outdoors (coats, winter hats, gloves) belong near the door (usually in a hall closet or on a coat rack). Organize your shoes wherever makes sense for you, depending on your habits and the layout of your home.

6 *Affordable Bedroom Upgrades That Won't Add Clutter*

If you're craving a new look for your bedroom but don't want to accumulate clutter (or spend a lot of cash), try some of these attractive, affordable, and organization-friendly options:

1. Switch up your drawer pulls, doorknobs, curtain rods, hooks, light switch covers, or furniture legs. They're there already—might as well make them more stylish.

2. Add a bed skirt. It can dress up a room while concealing less-than-appealing under-bed storage bins.

3. Install floating shelves. Put them over the bed or desk for easy access to your items, or on bare walls to add interest as well as storage space.

4. Use peel-and-stick wallpaper. This is the easiest way to add a pop of color or pattern and even totally change the look of a room without taking up any space at all.

5. Put your TV on the wall. Mounting a TV frees up space on your floor or console table.

6. Get a tissue box cover. It's one of the easiest small ways to make something mundane look intentional.

Try These Easy Ways to Separate a Bedroom in a Studio Apartment

When your bed*room* is more like a bed *corner*, it can be hard to separate sleep from work, meals, and hobbies. Have no fear—here are some ways to carve out dedicated space for your bedroom:

- **Use shelves to visually split the studio.** Place a bookcase (or two) between the bed and the living area. Decide which way you want to face the bookcase: The back side reads as a blank "wall" (that you can decorate—or not), while the open side provides storage for whatever area it faces.

- **Position a desk with built-in shelving as a border.** Depending on the desk's direction, you can make your home office part of either the bedroom or the living area.

- **Set up a screen or curtain.** This barrier can show off your personality and style, as well as hide your bedroom or reveal it whenever you choose.

Never Leave Your Bed

You live in a very small studio. You're sick. It's just too darn cold. For whatever reason, sometimes you just don't want to leave your bed—and that's okay! Here's how to stay under the covers *and* stay organized:

- **Get a bedside caddy.** This useful little catchall attaches to your bed (usually hanging from between the mattress and box spring) so books and small electronics are always within reach.

- **Turn a rolling cart into a bedside table.** These can be filled with what you need where you need (say, with snacks in the kitchen), then rolled into place. Stock with books, puzzles, art supplies, a mini-cooler, an electric kettle plus coffee and tea, or whatever you want.

Upgrade Your Kids' Bedrooms

Most bedroom organization advice applies to any bedroom, no matter the age of the person sleeping in it. But there are some special considerations in kids' rooms. Toys, for instance, present certain challenges; the concept of minimalism does not apply to stuffed animal collections. But there are still plenty of ways to wrangle all the precious items that kids own. Here are just a few ideas:

- **Store breakable things thoughtfully.** Under-bed drawers and shelves placed up high both maximize space, but the former lets kids access toys anytime they want, while the latter keeps fragile items in a safe spot.

- **Use storage cubes, boxes, and baskets for quick cleanup.** It's a lot easier—and faster—to toss toys into crates and cubbies than to place them in complicated original packaging or too-full drawers that don't open and close well. That's true whether you or your kid is doing the cleaning!

- **Label everything!** Slap a label on drawers, cubbies, pails, and anything else in your kids' rooms to distinguish what goes where or what belongs to which child. If they can't read yet, use images as labels.

- **Repurpose grown-up storage products for kid use.** Desk accessories intended for office supplies or fishing tackle boxes can hold tiny toys like LEGO bricks or beading supplies. Hanging shoe bags can also store small toys like action figures so you can see what's where, if your kid is tall enough to reach the slots. A hanging sweater bag can help you prep your kid's upcoming outfits. Just label the sections with the days of the week, then place folded clothes in each one.

- **Make stuffed animals multitask by stuffing them into a beanbag chair cover when not in use.** They're stored away out of sight and your kid has a cushy seat.

6 *Cool Ways to Use Bed Slats*

These adjoined strips of wood can do a lot more than just support a mattress. You can purchase them separately from some big-box stores or upcycle a set from a bed you're getting rid of. Use U-hooks to hang them on a wall, then try some of these clever tips:

1. Hang S-hooks over the slats to hold everything from purses to chunky necklaces to baseball caps.

2. Use two S-hooks to hang a wire basket and fill it with small office supplies, scrunchies, or anything you want.

3. Clip clothespins to the straps to display notes or photos.

4. Drape scarves, decorative textiles, or light blankets over the slats.

5. Hammer a few nails into the slats to hang a framed picture.

6. Attach a magnetic strip to a slat to hold hair pins or souvenir magnets.

Get creative and come up with your own ways to store or display your belongings!

Get Your Shoes in Line with Tension Rods

Too many shoes, not enough space? Join the club. Store more shoes by installing two tension rods, side by side and spaced a few inches apart, just above the floor of your closet. Measure the height first; you want to leave enough room for a row of shoes or boots underneath. Position tension rods flat for flat shoes, or place the back one slightly higher than the front for heeled shoes. (Heels will hang over the back rod while toes rest on the front one.) If you still have more shoes to stow, attach two more tension rods above the first set, again leaving enough room for shoes or boots to sit comfortably below.

Make Your Own Lap Desk

If you use your bed as a workspace, spot for breakfast, nail polishing location, or reading area, you might want a small flat surface to use. Take a basic shoe shelf, the kind that usually sits on the floor of a closet and comes with a top and bottom shelf. Remove (or don't install) the lower shelf, and you'll have essentially a horizontal desktop surface with two vertical supports. Sit on the bed, place the shelf over your lap, place your laptop on the shelf, and voilà: instant desk or table!

Bathroom

Don't Throw In the Towel

Bathrooms can be big or small, luxurious or utilitarian, beautiful or basic. But whatever they look like, every bathroom should be as *clean and comfortable* as possible. This chapter is full of cleaning hacks and organizing ideas that will help you get any kind of bathroom in order.

6 *Natural Alternatives to Harsh Bathroom Cleaners*

If store-bought bathroom cleaners leave you sneezy, dizzy, or woozy—or if you just want to save some cash—you can skip the name brands and make your own cleaning solutions. These mixtures use ingredients you probably already own:

1. All-purpose cleanser: Mix 1 cup of water with ½ cup of white vinegar in a spray bottle. Slowly stir in 2 tablespoons of baking soda, and the juice of half a lemon for optional fragrance.

2. Scouring powder: Mix equal parts baking soda, borax, and kosher salt.

3. Tub and shower cleaner: Combine 1½ cups of baking soda, ½ cup of water, ½ cup of liquid soap, and 2 tablespoons of white vinegar in a spray bottle.

4. Drain cleaner: Pour ½ cup of baking soda down the drain, then 1 cup of white vinegar. After 15 minutes (or overnight, if you like), flush with hot water.

5. Glass and chrome cleaner: Mix ¼ cup of white vinegar into 4 cups of water in a spray bottle. After spraying, wipe with a cloth or a crumpled sheet of newspaper for mirrors to avoid streaks.

6. Toilet bowl cleaner: Mix 2 cups of baking soda and 1 teaspoon of tea tree oil. To use, sprinkle a tablespoon or two into the bowl, then add 2 cups of white vinegar. Scrub, let sit for 15 minutes, then flush.

DIY

Take It from the Top

When cleaning your bathroom (or any space), start at the highest point in the room and work downward, leaving the floor for last. That way, any dust or dirt that drifts down will get mopped up in the final step.

Save Money and Reduce Waste with These Bathroom Product Hacks

These simple tips for common bathroom products will save you money, cut down on the amount of junk you throw away, reduce how much you need to buy, and cut your cleaning and organizing time. That's a win-win-win-win!

- When your bar of soap gets down to an unusable sliver, slather it together with another soap remnant or two.

- Get one reusable hand soap dispenser and buy a large refill-sized jug so you can restock as needed.

- When your shampoo, body lotion, and other products in plastic bottles and tubes seem to run out, cut open product containers with sturdy scissors and use a silicone spatula to find the hidden reservoir of product within.

- Use an all-purpose bathroom cleanser. Some of those specialized products do work really well, but don't resort to them unless your standard, everyday cleaning and disinfecting spray can't hack it.

- Use rags instead of paper towels. You'll save money, and they're better for the environment.

- Make your own cleaners. They cost less, and you can customize the scent profile using essential oils.

Switch Out Useless Fixtures

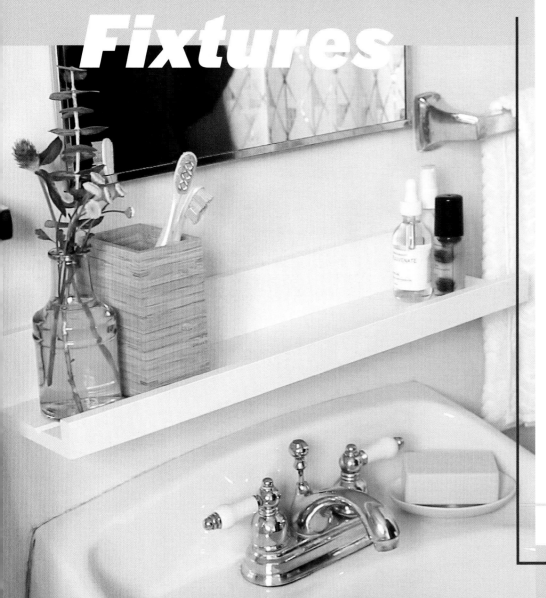

WHAT YOU NEED:

- Screwdriver
- Shelf with hanging hardware
- Drill and drill bits

DIY

They're the most annoying part of bathrooms that haven't been updated in ages: those little metal fixtures screwed above your sink that are supposed to hold toothbrushes and soap but just...don't. Today's toothbrushes are too thick to fit in those slots! To upgrade them, remove the holders and mountings with a screwdriver, and use the existing holes to install a floating shelf with a lip. Now you have a lot more over-sink space—and not just for toothbrushes and soap. This simple swap also makes up for the lack of counter space around a small sink, giving you room for a soap dispenser, nail brush, candle, or succulent.

HOW TO DO IT:

1. Remove old fixtures.

2. Remove any hardware or screws remaining. Tip: If you are renting, store all of these items together in a labeled bag.

3. Drill pilot holes into the shelf that match the holes already in the wall for the old fixtures.

4. Attach the shelf with screws.

5. Arrange any bathroom accessories you want on the shelf.

6 *Secretly Dirty Things You Need to Clean*

When you clean your bathroom, you know the toilet bowl, tub, sink, and floor are important. But make sure you're not inadvertently ignoring less obvious spots that can harbor not just dirt but all sorts of microscopic beasties you really don't want to share a bathroom with:

1. **The toilet handle:** That thing is just gross when you really think about it.

2. **Doorknobs, light switches, and drawer handles:** They're touched by everyone, all day, and no one ever thinks to wipe them clean.

3. **The showerhead:** Because the water that comes out of there drips directly onto your face.

4. **The floor behind the toilet:** Yeah, it's hard to reach, but that's no excuse to let it get nasty.

5. **The exterior of the toilet itself, including the tank:** It might not *look* dirty, but it probably is.

6. **Light fixtures:** If you never look at these till you have to change a light bulb, they'll end up absolutely coated in dust.

Keep Your Bathroom Reasonably Clean Every Day...

In general, you should be cleaning your bathroom at least once a week—though if a bathroom is used more frequently (or by a lot of people), it will need cleaning more often than one used less frequently (or by one person). The weekly cleaning should cover the toilet, shower/tub and tiles, sink, and floor. It's also a good time to take out the trash and change the towels (be sure to change the towels more than once a week, though!).

...But Don't Forget to Spring Clean It Too

Sure, you do your daily and weekly chores, but in order to get a *really* clean and organized bathroom, you will occasionally have to commit to a full-on deep-clean, aka spring cleaning. Here's how to do it:

- **Clear everything out.** Take all your products out of the shower and out from under the sink so you can really get at every surface. (Throw out anything expired, empty, or unwanted.) Also remove shower caddies and shelves, plus the shower curtain—including rings.

- **Scrub and sanitize everything with the appropriate products.** Clean and disinfect all surfaces and fixtures, the sink, toilet, tile walls, tub and shower, mirrors, windows...basically everything else you can get your gloved hands on. Clean the floors and wipe down the insides of cabinets.

- **Wash all linens.** That includes the shower curtain, towels, floor mats, and window curtains if you have them.

- **Wash any organizing products you'd removed earlier, then return them.** Now put all your stuff back neatly, decluttering if need be as you go. Wipe clean any product containers that have gotten grimy.

- **Air it out.** If you want to, open the window and light a candle to get that cleanser smell out and a fresh scent of your choice in.

   (Oh and btw, despite that *spring cleaning* term, you should actually plan to do this more than once a year!)

6 *Surprising Bathroom Cleaning Hacks*

If you need to clean the bathroom but you're out of your usual cleansers, you might be able to make do with an array of surprising (and mostly natural) items you already have sitting around:

1. Mirror cleaner: Steep three or four black tea bags in boiling water, then let the water cool and transfer to a spray bottle. Use the tea and water solution to naturally clean your dirty bathroom mirrors.

2. Disinfectant spray: Combine equal parts vodka and water to make a general disinfecting spray for bathroom floors, counters, and even those dirty crevices behind the toilet. Add essential oils to make the spray smell fresh.

3. Toilet bowl cleaner: Grab a pair of cleaning gloves and start scrubbing those hard-to-remove rings that form in your toilet bowl with a wet pumice stone.

4. Soap scum remover: To remove dried soap and water marks from a glass shower door, scrub with a wet dryer sheet, then rinse with water.

5. Metal hardware polish: Use a drop of baby oil to give metal hardware a shine. Just put some on a cloth and polish faucets and other fixtures after you clean them.

6. Tub cleaner: Scrub a bathtub with half a grapefruit generously sprinkled with salt, then rinse with water.

Understand What's Mold and What's Mildew

You might think they're just different names for the same icky fungi, but while mildew is common on damp surfaces (and easily removed), mold extends deeper and can cause serious health issues. Mildew is usually white or gray, while mold can be green or black.

Get Rid of Both Mold and Mildew

Once you've determined whether that stuff in your shower is mildew or mold, what should you do? First, always wear protective gear to shield yourself from harmful effects of harsh cleanser—or the mildew and mold themselves.

To clean mildew, you can use a commercial mildew remover, making sure the product is intended for tiles. Or mix equal parts white vinegar and lemon juice, then add baking soda to make a paste. Apply and scrub with a toothbrush, let sit for 5 minutes, then rinse with water.

If you suspect a serious mold infestation, call a professional. If it's a small amount, try treating it with a store-bought product. You can also attack mold with the usual natural heavy hitters: baking soda in water, tea tree oil in water, lemon juice, white vinegar, or hydrogen peroxide (not all at once!). Apply, wait, then wipe.

Clean Your Makeup Brushes

Cleaning makeup brushes can seem like a whole complicated thing these days, but you don't need specialized products and cleansers to keep your brushes sanitary. Try these quick and easy ways to keep brushes hygienic:

- To wash foundation brushes, wet with lukewarm water, then swirl them on a bar of unscented soap. Keep rinsing and swirling until the water runs clear.

- Clean eyeliner brushes by pouring a bit of olive oil on a clean towel, then rubbing the brush in the oil. Wash off with baby shampoo and warm water.

- To clean reusable makeup sponges, pour baby shampoo over the sponge, then squeeze under running water until the water runs clear.

- Clean brush handles with alcohol swabs, then let air-dry on a towel.

Take Care of Your Haircare Tools

If your hairstyling tools are looking a little worse for the wear, you can clean them with some simple DIY methods:

- To clean **wooden hairbrushes**, fill a small jar with water and add a few drops of tea tree oil. Remove any hair stuck in the brush, then use an old toothbrush to scrub the tea tree mixture onto the bristles. Swirl the brush in a bowl of warm water to rinse. Lay the brush bristles-down on a towel to dry.

- For **plastic or metal hair brushes**, mix water, a pinch of baking soda, and a squirt of castile soap. Remove any hair stuck in the brush, then use an old toothbrush to scrub the baking soda mixture onto the bristles. Swirl the brush in a bowl of warm water to rinse. Lay the brush bristles-down on a towel to dry.

- Unplug, then unscrew the back panel of your **hair dryer** and pull or twist it open. Clean dust from the mesh filter with an old toothbrush and soapy water. Let the filter dry on a paper towel, then reinsert.

- If your **curling iron or straightener** has a buildup of product on it, heat for 1 minute, then turn off and unplug. Mix one part rubbing alcohol and two parts baking soda, then apply the paste with an old toothbrush to the heating element. Let sit for 15 minutes. Brush the metal with the toothbrush and the ceramic with your fingers. Wipe the paste away with a washcloth.

5 **Creative Storage Solutions for Small Bathrooms**

If your bathroom is, shall we say, extra cozy (aka just really small), you might have to get creative when it comes to storage. Here are some ideas for maximizing the space you do have:

1. **Put shelves in the corner.** A triangular-shaped shelf snug in the corner will take up less space than a shelf of similar size along a wall.

2. **Look for a narrow over-the-toilet storage rack.** These are built to stand on the floor and fit around and above your toilet tank. If that style doesn't fit your space, mount a shelving unit or floating shelves on the otherwise wasted wall above the toilet.

3. **Squeeze into tiny spaces.** If there's a weird gap between your shower and sink, look for a skinny shelving unit that fits in there.

4. **Swap a mirror for a mirrored cabinet.** If the wall above your skink has a mirror without storage, install a medicine chest in its place. Even if it's a small one, every little bit helps!

5. **Roll in a cart.** Move it out of the way to let you fully open doors or clean certain areas, then move it back.

Organize Your Beauty Products

Here are some basic rules for simple bathroom beauty product organization:

- **Keep the products you use daily front and center.** Your face wash should be easy to reach anytime; a clay mask you use every few months can go on the top shelf or at the back.

- **Store like with like.** Keep hair products together, face products together, and so on. (Extend this to other bathroom items like first aid supplies and shaving things.)

- **Use lidded jars or other matching clear containers for cotton balls, cotton swabs, and so on.** They're clear so you can see what's where, and matching so they stand side by side without wasting space.

- **Use multiple sizes of containers.** To keep beauty products upright, corral them either in large containers divided into sections, or smaller ones grouped together.

Magnetize Your Storage

Attach a magnetic strip to the inside of your medicine cabinet door. No more losing track of bobby pins, nail clippers, tweezers, and other tiny metal things!

Remove Scuffs from Walls

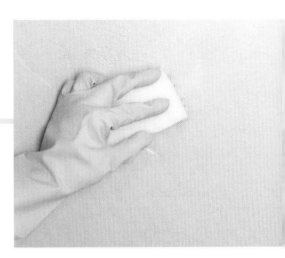

When formerly spotless walls start looking scuffed, spot-treat those dingy streaks with a Magic Eraser.

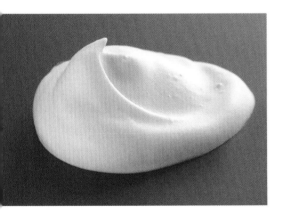

Try This Old-School Mirror Cleaning Hack

This vintage cleaning tip is perfect in a pinch: Polish your bathroom mirror by slathering it with a little foam shaving cream and wiping clean with a cloth.

Get That Lime Off

To remove lime buildup from your showerhead, fill a small plastic bag with white vinegar, then attach it with a rubber band so the showerhead is completely submerged. Do the same for your sink and tub faucets. For sink and tub drains, close the stopper and pour in enough vinegar to cover it. Let sit overnight, then scrub with a brush and rinse with water.

Keep Extra Trash Bags Right Where You Need 'Em

If you've never seen this hack in action before, prepare to be amazed: Store a stash of trash can liners at the bottom of the can. Next time you take out the trash, you can pop in a fresh liner right away.

Keep These Bathroom Cleaning Supplies Handy

What do you need to have on hand to fully clean your bathroom? The list will vary slightly depending on your preferences and your space, but it will generally look something like this.

- Cleaning gloves
- Sponges
- Rags or paper towels
- Disinfectant wipes
- Toilet brush
- Scrub brush
- Old toothbrush
- Toilet bowl cleaner
- Tub and tile cleaner
- All-purpose cleaner and disinfectant spray
- Glass cleaner
- Vacuum
- Wet/dry mop
- Trash bags

Organize Your Bathroom Cleaning Products

Cleaning your bathroom is a priority, and it's easier to do when the products you use are stored nearby. Here are some guidelines:

- **Minimize the number of products you use.** The less you have, the less space it takes up, and the less cluttered everything looks. Look for cleaners that can do double duty.

- **Keep it together.** Store bathroom cleansers in one box or drawer. This way, you'll never have to wonder where you put that one spray bottle.

- **Standardize containers.** If you're refilling from larger containers or making your own cleansers, keep products in (labeled) bottles of the same shape and size. That way, they'll fit together on a shelf or in a caddy more easily.

- **Corral them in a cupboard.** Keep products together with a caddy, rack, tray, or basic plastic bin. This separates them from other products you keep nearby, helps limit damage from leaks or spills, and means you can easily grab the products to clean another bathroom if you have more than one.

Restore Dingy Grout

You know how some tile floors just never look clean, no matter how well you mop them? It might be that the grout has gotten stained. Grab a grout pen and trace over your grout lines—it's as easy to use as a marker and restores that "new tile look" like scrubbing never will.

Scrub the Tub Without Hurting Your Back

If you've been bending over to scrub your tub and you're just not about that life anymore, try this: Drizzle dish soap all around the tub, add a little water to get some bubbles going, then use a clean broom with stiff bristles to scrub as you stand. When you've scrubbed the surfaces clean, run the shower to wash away the suds.

Prevent Clogged Drains

One of the nastiest bathroom chores is dealing with a clogged shower drain. Nip that horror in the bud by using a drain cover. This little mesh thingamajig traps hair before it gets into the drain, meaning less gross work for you.

Give Rubber Duckies Their Own Bath

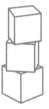

To clean kids' bath toys, soak them for 10 minutes in 1 gallon of water mixed with ½ cup of white vinegar. Rub with a sponge, then air-dry. (Squeeze out excess water to prevent mold.) To store toys, attach a plastic tub with drainage holes and suction cups to the tile wall.

5 Common Shower Storage Issues and How to Address Them

If storing products in your shower is making it feel cramped or messy, fear not. There's a simple shower organization solution no matter what your storage issue:

1. **Lots of squeeze bottles in your shower?** Install a tension rod and use shower rings with clips attached to hold the flat ends of the bottles.

2. **No shower shelf space?** Hang a caddy over the showerhead or in the corner for easy-to-reach shelving.

3. **Shared shower?** Get each person a plastic bin or caddy to fill with their own products.

4. **Shampoo bottles, razors, and soap constantly tumbling off the edge of the tub?** Here's a magical thing that exists: shower curtains with pockets.

5. **Shower looking like a storeroom?** Don't store backup products there. Reserve shower storage for only those things you use daily—or weekly—and keep extra or occasionally used products elsewhere.

Decide What to Store Where

Finding a home for everything you own is an organizing must. So if you have more storage space outside your bathroom (say, in a bedroom or hall closet), how should you decide what to store where?

- **Ask yourself where you use the item.** Do you habitually deposit your dirty clothes in the bathroom or in the bedroom? Your answer will tell you where to put the laundry hamper.

- **Consider conditions.** The bathroom feels like a convenient spot for nail polish, but the humidity and temperature fluctuations can make it break down faster.

- **Think about square footage.** If you have a tiny bathroom and a large linen closet, your space is essentially making the decision for you—keep your extra towels in the linen closet.

Measure Before You Organize

Peek into the mess that is the cabinet under your bathroom sink, and you'll probably get the urge to run to the nearest homeware store and stock up on organizers. But take a minute to measure first, because it's all too easy to buy a bunch of bins, then get home to find they don't actually fit on the shelf you wanted to use. Or they fit, but your stuff doesn't fit in them. So before you commit, measure both your shelves and the stuff you're trying to straighten out.

7 Cool Ways to Store Your Towels

You just got a new set of soft, fluffy towels. Where are you going to store them? (Hint: not the floor!) Depending on your bathroom layout and style, there are countless possibilities.

1. Bars: the classic option. Mount a bar on the back of the door or on a wall; for a twist, mount another bar vertically and store dry, rolled-up towels in a row behind it.

2. Hooks: super simple. Slip some over the door, no tools required, or mount them on the door or wall.

3. Racks or stands: the versatile choice. Racks come in all shapes, styles, and sizes and can hold other supplies along with towels.

4. Baskets: easy and pretty. Baskets can rescue an otherwise awkward bathroom by carving out effortless-looking storage areas in any corner.

5. Shelves: endlessly customizable. Depending on your space, you could pick anything from a couple small floating shelves to a larger unit like a hutch or bookcase.

6. Cubbies: cute and combinable. Place them high on the wall to use vertical space in a small bathroom, or down on the floor to make dry towels accessible to kids.

7. Ladders: a space saver. Whether hanging from the wall or leaned against it, a ladder-style towel holder can store a lot without taking up too much room.

Keep Makeup in Another Spot

One thing you shouldn't store in the bathroom, if you can avoid it, is makeup. The humidity and temperature fluctuations break down ingredients and invite bacteria. Instead, store it in a cool, dry place. If you do your makeup in the bathroom, store your daily go-tos in a caddy or makeup bag for easy access. (Makeup remover, however, is fine in your bathroom.)

Branch Out When Decorating

When decorating and organizing your bathroom, don't feel that you need to stick to typical bathroom furniture and accessories. Sometimes items meant for other rooms end up being the most useful and attractive options. For example, you might:

- Hang your bathrobe using over-the-door hooks sold for a coat closet.
- Find a nightstand or kitchen stool that perfectly holds products for your bath.
- Use a small bookshelf to stack towels.
- Arrange face creams and lotions in an organizer from your office or on a lazy Susan from the kitchen.

Keep an open mind and browse different sections of the store.

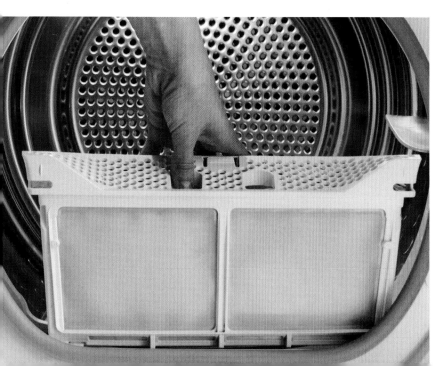

CHAPTER 6

Laundry Room

Wash, Dry, Fold, Organize

Love it or hate it, laundry is one of those things you just have to do. The following pages are full of advice on **how to clean your clothes** and how to organize your space so your laundry room works with you, not against you. No matter what your feelings are on laundry, you can get the satisfaction that comes from getting it done **right** and checking it off your to-do list.

6 Old-Fashioned Laundry Tricks

People have been cleaning clothes since time immemorial, but our ancestors sure weren't using neon goop in plastic pods. Here are some time-tested laundry tips:

1. To make your own all-natural detergent, combine $2\frac{1}{4}$ cups of water, 1 cup of liquid castile soap, $\frac{3}{4}$ cup of baking soda, and $\frac{1}{4}$ cup of salt in a large jar. Use $\frac{1}{4}$ cup of the mixture per load.

2. Use baking soda, which, unsurprisingly, is a must-have in the laundry room. To whiten whites and generally get clothes cleaner, add some to your regular wash. To get rid of odors on sweaty-smelling shirts, make a paste with baking soda and water, scrub it on, and let sit overnight before washing. Or dissolve a cup or two of baking soda in warm water, then add that along with the stinky clothes to a tub of cool water, and let soak overnight before washing.

3. Speed up drying time by throwing a clean, dry towel in the machine with your damp clothes.

4. Add hydrogen peroxide to your wash to whiten white clothes, or mix some with water to brighten bright clothes. Pour a little on clothing to treat blood or food stains, then let sit for 10 minutes before washing. (And remember: Never mix hydrogen peroxide with other household chemicals—it will be useless at best, dangerous at worst.)

5. Do a load of laundry with $\frac{1}{2}$ cup of white vinegar in place of detergent to clean and deodorize clothing. Or pretreat stains with a solution of 1 cup of vinegar per 1 gallon of water.

6. Wash colored clothes inside out to prevent fading.

Air-Dry Clothes Without a Line or Rack

If you want to let your clothes dry naturally—whether to save money or energy, because your dryer is broken, or because the item can't be machine-dried—it obviously helps to have a nice clothesline hanging in your backyard. Failing that, the go-to indoor option is a drying rack. But how can you dry everything properly with no rack? Use your furniture! Drape dry towels over your stairway banister and straight-backed chairs to convert them to makeshift drying racks. You can also place towels on beds and floors and lay clothing flat to dry. Other items can be hung by the clips on pant hangers; just don't do this with anything delicate.

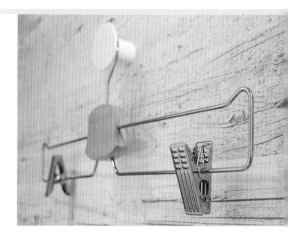

Unshrink Shrunken Clothes

Oops, you did it again. You put that top in the dryer that *really* shouldn't have gone in the dryer, and now it's cropped circa early 2000s fashion. But before you relegate it to a pop star Halloween costume, try this fix.

In a bowl or sink, mix 1 tablespoon of hair conditioner into 1 quart of warm water. Add your shrunken garment, make sure it's saturated, then let it soak for 30 minutes. Gently squeeze out the water, without wringing out the garment, and lay it flat on a clean towel. Roll up the garment in the towel while pressing to get rid of excess moisture. Stretch the garment on another clean towel, using clothespins to clip it at the edges, then let the garment air-dry.

Be Kind to the Planet with Eco-Friendly Laundry Tips

Want to swap some of your old laundry products and practices for ones that are kinder to the environment? Luckily, there are lots of options, some new and some old-school:

- **Eco-friendly laundry detergent** acts just like regular detergent, but it's made without certain chemicals that are harmful to the environment—and, potentially, to you. It may also be made with packaging that reduces waste and especially reduces the use of plastic.

- **Biodegradable laundry detergent pods** provide natural detergent in Earth-friendly, individually sized bubbles.

- **All-natural laundry tablets** are sustainable and easy to use; just add one to water for instant eco-friendly detergent, sans plastic packaging.

- **Soap nuts** are not nuts, but actually dried berries from the *Sapindus mukorossi* tree, which do contain a type of natural soap. They're gentle, reusable, and compostable, and can be grown without pesticides.

- **Wool dryer balls** do the same job as fabric softener, as well as shortening drying time. And not only are they all-natural, but you can reuse them for ages.

- **Air-drying** is a green alternative to the dryer. Hang your clothes on a clothes-line or drying rack, and you'll save money on energy and reduce your carbon footprint.

- **At-home laundering** will let you skip the trip to the dry cleaner. Dry cleaners often use damaging chemicals, so limit dry cleaning by caring for your clothes well, treating stains yourself when you can, and buying pieces that don't require dry cleaning.

De-Pill Your Sweaters

Sad as it may look, a pilled sweater is not beyond help. You can remove pills from sweaters and other items with a battery-operated fabric shaver, a disposable razor, small scissors, a pumice stone, or a sweater comb.

Stop Losing Laundry

If you use the top of your washer and dryer to rest or fold piles of laundry, get a laundry guard. This plastic rail sticks magnetically to the top of your appliances so clothes can't slip over the back and sides.

Write a Reminder

Hang a small chalkboard in your laundry room. Whenever you put a load in the washer, jot down any items that can't go in the dryer. You'll remind yourself, and anyone else who might move the laundry from the washer to the dryer.

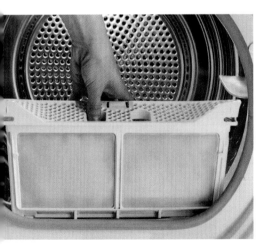

Clean the Lint Trap!

You probably do this anyway, because your mom told you to. But this isn't just a weird parent thing. If you don't do it, your house could catch fire. You're welcome!

6 Common Summertime Stains and How to Get Rid of Them

Warm weather is so much fun—until it gets all over your clothes. Here's how to treat typical clothing stains from outdoor activities:

1. Barbecue sauce: Turn the garment inside out and hold it under cold water. Add liquid detergent, let it sit for 10 minutes, then rinse. Gently blot with white vinegar and rinse. Repeat the detergent/rinse/vinegar/rinse until most of the stain is gone. Add pretreater stick or spray, then wash as usual.

2. Sweat: Rub the garment with bar soap before washing. If the area is discolored, soak in white vinegar and hot water. Wash as usual on the hottest setting the garment allows.

3. Sunscreen: Apply pretreater or liquid detergent directly to the stain and rub it in. Wash as usual on the hottest setting the garment allows.

4. Iced tea: Dab with cold water from the reverse side of the stain. Soak in cold water mixed with detergent for 30 minutes or overnight. Wash as usual.

5. Fruit juice: Pretreat with strong detergent, then rinse. If the stain is still there, soak in equal parts cold water and bleach for 30 minutes. Wash as usual.

6. Ice cream: Soak in cold water for 10 minutes. Add dish detergent and let sit for 30 minutes. Rinse and wash as usual.

If the garment is still stained after washing, don't put it in the dryer! Instead, soak in a mixture of equal parts hydrogen peroxide and water, then wash again.

Try These Tricks for Tough Stains

For every possible stain, there's a different (and often unexpected) stain removal solution. The next time you find your favorite outfit covered in some unusual substance, try one of these laundry hacks:

- For tomato-based stains, soak the garment and hang it—still very wet—in the sun.

- To treat a lipstick stain on fabric, blot with soft white bread, then wash.

- Vanquish ink stains with either hairspray or hand sanitizer. Just cover, let sit for 10 minutes, then wash.

- Grease stain? Rub chalk into it to absorb the oil. Or sprinkle baby powder on the stain, then brush off. Wash as usual.

- Remove an acrylic paint stain with rubbing alcohol. Then wash.

- Banish foundation from clothing by adding shaving cream to the stain and letting it sit for 30 minutes. Then just wash as usual.

Set a Laundry Timer

You're a busy person with things to do; you can't just *remember* when your laundry is going to be finished. Set an alarm on your phone so you don't let wet laundry sit in a damp lump while dry laundry goes around and around and around for all eternity.

Make a Hanging Laundry Organizer

WHAT YOU NEED:

- 2 U-hooks
- Twin-sized bed slats
- Scissors

A set of bed slats hung from a wall is both a creative space saver and an attractive way to organize your laundry necessities. You can buy bed slats separately from a big-box store or upcycle them from a bed you're getting rid of.

HOW TO DO IT:

1. Screw both U-hooks into the wall at the height you want.

2. Hang bed slats from the hooks.

3. Cut the straps to your desired length. (Leaving some space between the last slat and the floor makes room for, say, hanging clothes off the last slat.)

4. When the slats are in place, arrange your items however you like:

- Hang extra clothes hangers from the U-hooks.

- Hang spray bottles over the slats.

- Hang a piece of string between two pushpins and use clothespins to turn one slat into a lost-and-found for stray socks.

- Place S-hooks over the slats to hang wire baskets holding glass jars of dryer sheets, detergent pods, or found coins. You can also hang a small steamer, lint roller, or mini–ironing board this way.

5 Ways to Make Your Trip to the Laundromat Less of a Hassle

If your laundry day involves lugging your clothes to and from your building's basement laundry room or the laundromat down the street, these tips and ideas can make the chore feel a little less like, well, a chore:

1. Get a wheeled shopping cart. They're built to hold a lot of stuff, and you can fold them up for easy storage.

2. Separate clothes before you go. You'll roll up at the laundromat with your laundry already sorted and ready to dump into the machines.

3. Consider a stair-climbing cart. Look for a rolling cart with special wheels designed to trek up steps. Life-changing!

4. Get a hamper that's also a backpack. A laundry bag with back straps makes for easier transportation.

5. Portion out detergent at home. Avoid lugging a box, bottle, or tub by pouring the correct amount of powder detergent or pods into a zip-top plastic bag, or liquid detergent into a small plastic container.

Do Laundry Less Often

If you, like most people, consider laundry to be a massive pain, you might prefer to simply do it as infrequently as you can. Here's how:

- Don't wash when you don't need to. If you wear something for only a few hours, it might be perfectly fine to rewear without washing.
- Treat stains quickly. If you fully remove a small stain, you may not need to wash the whole garment.
- Buy extra underwear, socks, workout clothes, and other things that need washing every time.
- Wear T-shirts under sweaters and sweatshirts so you can rewear the heavier pieces multiple times between washings.

Keep Your Sneakers Looking Fresh-Out-of-the-Box Clean

Most athletic shoes, whether leather or fabric, can go in the washing machine. (Always check labels first, though!) Before washing your sneakers, remove any dirt and debris that you can brush away, and remove the laces. Most laces can be washed in the machine, using bleach first to treat stains if necessary. (Also take out the insoles, if they're removable, and scrub them with baking soda and water.) Then, put your shoes in the wash in warm water on a regular cycle. You might want to add some towels to balance the load, and use a mesh bag. Leather shoes shouldn't go in the dryer, but many cotton and canvas sneakers can—just check the label on your pair to be sure. To be safe, air-dry laces and sneakers to prevent shrinkage.

If you don't want to put your sneakers in the washer, clean them by hand with a soft brush (a toothbrush will do), water, and gentle liquid laundry detergent.

Maximize Space in a Small Laundry Room

In a little laundry area, it can be hard to store the things you need and do all those laundry-adjacent tasks. Here are some ways to make the most of that space:

- If your laundry room has a door—or if there's a nearby closet door that will work—use an over-the-door hanging organizer to hold bottles of detergent, dryer sheets, and everything else you need.

- Install a shelf high up on a wall. If you've got an empty wall above your washer and dryer, or nearby, use that available vertical space for a floating shelf to hold supplies.

- Skip the trash can and put a little magnetic waste bin on your dryer to deposit lint.

- If there's no room for an upright steamer, get a handheld travel steamer.

- Choose a collapsible drying rack, whether it stands on the floor or hangs on the back of a door. Then fold it flat and put it away when it's not in use.

- Get a multi-clip hanger for drying small clothing items, and you won't need extra surface space to dry them flat.

- If you have more wall space than surface space, install a hanging rack for detergents and mount your ironing board on the wall along with a basket to hold your iron and spray starch.

- Slide a skinny shelf between your washer and dryer.

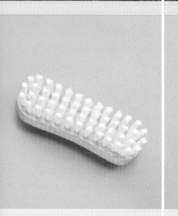

9 *Little Products That Make Doing Laundry Easier*

Sometimes laundry just goes easier with a little help from some cool products. If you're not satisfied with your laundry routine, look for these the next time you shop:

1. Reusable mesh laundry bags to protect delicate items and keep socks together in the washer and dryer.

2. Sock clips to prevent half of a pair from wandering off.

3. A clothing folder, which is basically training wheels for anyone who just can't get the hang of folding stuff neatly.

4. A dryer vent cleaning brush, aka a narrow, bendy thingy to get in every lint-filled crevice of your dryer.

5. A baseball cap washer to keep your cap collection in perfect shape as you run them through the dishwasher. (You do know to wash caps in the dishwasher, right?)

6. Anti-vibration pads for your washer and dryer. These rubber "feet" slip under your appliances to prevent them from shaking themselves halfway across the room.

7. A mesh sneaker bag to protect your shoes in the washer and hold them in place in the dryer.

8. A stain brush just for laundry so you don't have to steal the scrub brush from the kitchen or bathroom.

9. A wall-mounted dryer sheet dispenser to make it easier to grab a sheet; it also frees up surface space and makes your laundry room look fancy.

Get That Gross Dye Smell Out of Jeans

Have you ever gotten a new pair of black jeans home, only to discover that they smell like something went terribly wrong in a chemical factory? That's formaldehyde, and it can linger in fabric for a long time. To fully fade that eye-watering odor, turn jeans inside out to lessen fading. Then try these options:

- Try just hanging jeans in fresh air.

- If that doesn't work, try machine-washing or soaking in cold water and either baking soda, borax, castile soap, or white vinegar.

- You can also try an oxygen bleach wash; follow the directions on the product you choose.

Keep Your Laundry Area Clean

Even though it's usually a small room (or not even a room at all), you still have to clean your laundry area!

- Wash floors and wipe or dust surfaces as you would anywhere, and pay extra attention to stray lint.

- What with all that soap, you'd think your washer wouldn't have to be cleaned, but it does! Just add 2 cups of hydrogen peroxide and run the washer on hot. Or follow the same process with 1 cup of white vinegar. You can even buy commercially available wipes for washing machines!

- You can clean your (cool, unplugged) iron with a paste of baking soda and water. Scrub gently, then wipe clean with a cloth dampened in white vinegar.

- Don't forget to wash your fabric ironing board cover once in a while.

6 Items That Can Level Up Your Laundry Room Look

These items—some big, some small—can really make a laundry area feel functional and adult-looking.

1. A tension rod: Install a custom-sized hanging rod for newly ironed clothes or clothes that need airing out.

2. A countertop: If you have two front-loading machines side by side, placing a countertop or flat board across them can give you a convenient workspace for folding clothes, resting a laundry basket, or any other task.

3. Measuring cups: Sure, you have them in your kitchen. But your laundry deserves its own set of cups for detergent and any other powder or liquid you might need to measure.

4. A tall woven basket with a lid: It's classic, rustic, and pretty enough to not be hidden in the closet.

5. Eco-friendly laundry products: You'll feel better about lessening your impact on the environment and, as a bonus, these products often come in subtler packaging than the typical detergents.

6. Proper laundry area lighting: Come on, stop using your phone's flashlight to find your washer and dryer in your dark basement.

Set Laundry Apart When It's Combined with Another Room

If your laundry room is essentially a small section of another room in your home, there are two main ways to make the setup look seamless: You can either conceal the washer and dryer as much as possible, or blend both sections of the room intentionally using decor and organization.

To hide a laundry area, consider curtains, louvered folding doors, or a sliding door. Look for any unused vertical space or empty corners where you can incorporate floating shelves or hanging baskets.

To make it work while keeping everything in the open, cut way back on clutter, stick with the same colors and textures throughout, and, if possible, double up on storage areas. For example, a shelving unit between the kitchen and laundry area can hold both items for both areas.

Roll In a Utility Cart

There is no part of the house where a rolling cart can't be of use, and the laundry room is no exception. A cart with two or three shelves can hold just about everything you need: Use the lower levels for detergent and other products, and rest your laundry basket on top. In an awkwardly shaped room, the wheels let you move the cart out of the way to swing open your dryer door. And because you can find a utility cart in almost any color (or spray-paint one a custom color to personalize it even further!), it can be cute as well as practical.

CHAPTER

7

Workspace

Home Sweet Office

Whether you **work from home** full-time, run a home-based side hustle, or just periodically have emails to answer and bills to pay, your living space needs an area dedicated to getting stuff done. When you create a comfortable, clean, and clutter-free working area, you'll feel way *more productive*!

Embrace a "Less Is More" Philosophy

Whether you're setting up a new workspace or refreshing an existing one, it's important to remember: Less stuff equals more productivity. In other words, you need to declutter.

Once you identify and eliminate unnecessary items, you'll be less distracted by the visual clutter that leads to procrastination. You'll also spend far less time cleaning. Of course, you can still store the supplies you really need; the key is keeping them organized, accessible, and preferably out of sight.

Here's the thing: Decluttering is not a one-time project. You will have to do it semi-regularly. But starting off right means it will soon become second nature to keep your work area clutter-free.

Clean Your Desk, Clear Your Mind

Humans are easily distracted. Fight that "Oh, look, a squirrel!" energy by cleaning off your desk or work surface as much as you possibly can. Work is hard enough without fifty-seven gadgets and decorations fighting for your attention.

Lights, Camera, Work!

If you've ever tried to read a computer screen in front of a window on a sunny day, you know that lighting is crucial in a workspace. Choose an area of your home with (preferably adjustable) natural or artificial light that helps, rather than hinders, your work.

Prioritize Concentration

The best, cleanest, and most impeccably organized office won't get used if it's unpleasantly loud or otherwise distracting. When setting up your workspace, think about how you can avoid or mitigate outside noise.

Consider Flexibility

Pro tip: You don't actually have to work in your workspace. Some people feel more motivated at a desk; others get a ton done on the couch. However, your work *stuff*—whether that's camera equipment or reference books—deserves a home where you can always find it.

Try a Portable Office Option

If you don't have the space for even the tiniest home office, or if you just prefer to work in different spots throughout the day, you can still give your work supplies a home and bring your workspace with you. Use a basket or caddy with a handle, or a rolling cart. Collect the things you need—like your laptop, notebooks, pens, planner, and so on—and put them in your portable "office." When you switch from the couch to the kitchen table, just pick up your caddy or roll your cart along with you. To keep your things organized, just make it a habit to put everything away at the end of your workday, and do a regular declutter to make sure you're not carting around any old mail or dried-up pens.

5 Items to Declutter from Your Home Office

If your office feels cramped or looks messy, there's a good chance it's time to declutter. Here are some categories to consider as you sort through the stuff:

1. Office supplies: Look for items you no longer use (ancient bottles of Wite-Out), anything that's broken (calculators that don't calculate), and things you feel you "should" keep but have no use for (fancy stationery).

2. Furniture: If you have a chair no one ever sits on, removing it will instantly free up a ton of space.

3. Tech: Get rid of chargers that don't charge, cables with no corresponding appliance, and any power cord that looks frayed or damaged. If you're feeling ambitious, deal with that stack of old laptops and tiny phones from the cellular Stone Age.

4. Purely decorative items: Choose two or three you definitely want to keep, then consider rehoming the rest, or at least moving them to other parts of the house.

5. Old files, papers, magazines, and business cards: Paper clutter can take the longest to finally deal with, but it's totally worth your time and effort.

Maintain a Clutter-Free Home Office

Let's say you've organized your workspace, it looks great, and you feel extra productive...for a month, at least, at which point it all falls apart. How can you prevent this? Here are some tips:

- **Shop consciously.** Before you buy anything, stop and ask yourself whether you truly need it.

- **Create a routine for dealing with mail, packages, and other items that can easily accumulate in your workspace.** Set up a system—this could just be a simple in-box and out-box—to help you process it all efficiently.

- **Stay on top of paper waste.** If you need a shredder and an office recycling bin to dispose of papers, get them.

- **Digitize when you can.** Some things will always need to be on paper, but if you're just holding on to hard copies out of laziness, start scanning!

Declutter Your Documents

Dealing with paper can be daunting. It's not just that filing is boring—it's also fraught with uncertainty: What might the IRS come looking for in ten years? To make filing go faster, look up the guidelines for every type of paperwork your job (and life) requires. They'll mostly fit into one of three categories: documents you do not need and can safely shred; documents you do need, but not necessarily in physical form; and documents you need to keep as hard copies.

Once you clarify the rules, sort through those papers. Shred what can go, then file (in a manila folder or a computer folder, depending on the info you found) and label what needs to stay. Then write down the filing rules and stick them securely inside your file cabinet or box, so you'll never again have to wonder how long to keep anything.

Dust This Room Too

While you're cleaning your desk, keep in mind that you also have to clean the rest of your workspace (floor, shelves, wastebasket) just as you'd clean any other room in the house. It might not get visibly dirty like the kitchen, but it's low-key covered in dust.

Clean These Items in Your Workspace

Maybe it's spring, maybe your workspace is looking extra chaotic after a big project, or maybe you just want to give your whole home a good scrubbing. Here's a checklist to run through when you're deep-cleaning your home office:

- Your desk or other work surface—inside the drawers too
- Desk accessories
- Your computer, phone, and other tech or equipment, including your computer mouse if you have one
- The floor and any rugs or carpets on it
- Light fixtures, from desk lamps to ceiling lights
- Corners, windowsills, blinds, ceiling fans, under chairs and tables, and any other places where dust collects
- Shelves, whether they're mounted on the wall or part of a larger shelving unit
- Other furniture, like tables or chairs
- Storage areas for supplies

- Any other spaces you work in beyond your desk and "office" area, such as a studio or crafting space

- The wastebasket and recycling bin

- Light switches, doorknobs, and other frequently touched, germ-harboring spots

- Fabrics and upholstery, if applicable: curtains, chair cushions, and so on

- Paper (This is not the kind of "cleaning" you can do with a dust mop or all-purpose cleanser, but nothing makes an office feel cleaner than tackling stacks of stray papers. Shred, recycle, or file them so you can actually clean the surfaces underneath.)

4 Ways to Clean Your Smartphone

Your phone—yes, the one that's constantly in your hand, touching your face, and sitting beside you when you eat—is a breeding ground for bacteria. Seriously, it's utterly filthy. Power down your phone and try one of these ways to clean and disinfect it:

1. To disinfect, mix equal parts distilled water and rubbing alcohol in a small spray bottle. Spray onto a microfiber cloth and wipe carefully. (For even easier cleaning, use alcohol wipes.) Don't just do the screen—make sure to get the back, sides, and case as well.

2. To clear prints and smudges from your screen, wipe with a microfiber cloth in one direction until all residue is gone.

3. To clean an extra-grimy phone, mix equal parts water and white vinegar in a small spray bottle. Spray onto a microfiber cloth and wipe in one direction until all residue is gone.

4. To get all high-tech about it, wipe away fingerprints and residue with a microfiber cloth. Then hold a UV light $2\frac{1}{2}$ to 3 inches above your phone screen for 10 to 15 seconds in each place. Repeat until each area has been covered.

Take Care of Your Computer

No, this is not about wiping your hard drive. It's about making sure the outside of your computer is free of dust and dirt (and crumbs, no judgment). There are many cool-looking little gadgets sold for this purpose, but as with most household tasks, it works just as well if you keep it simple.

- Turn off and unplug your computer. Slightly dampen a microfiber cloth with water and wipe the exterior. You never want too much water, or any liquid, on or in your computer, so be careful!

- Wipe the screen gently, first with a dry cloth and then with one that's slightly damp with a mixture of equal parts water and white vinegar.

- Clean your keyboard using a slightly damp cloth, a can of compressed air, and a cotton swab dampened with rubbing alcohol. You can also clean a mouse with rubbing alcohol (unplug and/or remove the batteries first).

Sort Through Your Pens

Here's a mindless task you can do in minutes to feel a lot better about your workspace: Go through all the pens you've accumulated and throw out any that don't work. Put the rest in a cute container—or better, two: one for ballpoints and one for highlighters or colored markers.

Find Space under Your Desk

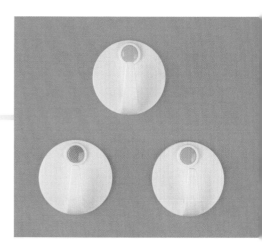

If your desk lacks drawers and always ends up covered with small necessities like headphones and pens, look for organizers like stick-on hooks and small drawers that slide under your desktop.

Color-Coordinate Your Materials

Use color-coded file folders, sticky notes, and envelopes to get your stuff in order. Sticking to a limited color palette overall makes any space look cleaner and neater, so go with subtle variations or different patterns within the same range of colors.

Use a Backseat Organizer on Your Office Chair

Squeeze more storage into a teeny workspace with a backseat organizer made to hold road trip supplies or distractions for kids. You can fit a surprising number of small items like pens, sticky notes, earbuds, and chargers without taking up an inch of precious desk space.

Keep an Inventory of Your Supplies

No matter what supplies you need to do your job—stamps, printer ink, memory cards—you're going to run out of them eventually. To keep on top of your office supplies, as well as other stuff you go through in your workspace, like tissues or hard candy, you have to keep tabs on your inventory. The first step is to organize what you do have, in a place where you'll know to look for it. Once that's done, you'll be able to see when something's getting low and add it to your shopping list. Organizing supplies also means you won't accidentally buy too much.

Hide Cords and Wires

BEFORE

AFTER

WHAT YOU NEED:

- Floating picture ledge with hardware
- Drill with a large drill bit (e.g., 1½ inches)
- Power strip

Cords hanging off your desk and snaking across your floor can make even the neatest office space look sloppy. Here's a way to conceal those cables using a floating picture ledge.

HOW TO DO IT:

1. Drill a large hole into the shelf of a floating picture ledge.

2. Attach the shelf to your wall above an outlet.

3. Run the cord of a power strip through the hole, then plug it into the outlet.

4. Rest the power strip on the picture ledge, plug your electronics into the power strip, and move a piece of furniture in front of it, concealing the whole thing.

If your phone's charging cable is too short, leaving your phone dangling from the outlet, cut an empty plastic bottle in half so the phone fits inside. Use a craft knife to cut a square the size of a phone charger into the back. Stick the charger through the hole and plug it in so your phone can charge while resting safely, cable and all, on the outlet but inside the holder.

5 Steps to Organizing a Messy Desk

If looking at your desk kinda makes you want to cry, you can fix it in a lot less time than you think! Follow these steps to de-mess a desk:

1. Get a trash bag to throw away anything you come across that belongs in the garbage.

2. Take everything off your desk and wipe the surface clean. (Though you don't have to, you'll feel extra productive if you also wipe electronics, dust lights, and clean the floor around the desk.)

3. Put back only the items that need to be there. This means only those things you use regularly at your desk. Organize everything on your desktop, in the drawers, and so on. If you haven't already designated places for specific items, do that while you organize.

4. Deal with the items that didn't make it back to your desk. If they're work-related things, put them where they belong (say, in a file or on a shelf). If they're stray things, return them to the kitchen, living room, or wherever they should live.

5. Finally, consider any issues that caused your desk to get messy in the first place and make a plan to sort that out. Maybe you just need a larger set of drawers to keep things from spilling over, or maybe you need to establish a nightly routine of taking coffee mugs back to the kitchen when you're done working so they don't multiply on your desk.

Use a Wall for Organizing

If you're trying to get creative with storage in a small space, or if you're just trying to keep as much stuff off your desk as possible, the answer might be staring you in the face. Yes, it's your blank wall. You can use a wall to hang nearly anything you might put on a shelf or desktop. For example:

- Hang wire storage baskets or install floating shelves.

- Choose a wall calendar and clock over their deskbound counterparts.

- Use a bulletin board to display important notes.

- Clip clothespins to twine to string up photos or little pieces of art that would otherwise need a surface and a frame.

- Put a pegboard above your desk and hang scissors and tape dispensers from it.

    The possibilities are almost endless!

Get in the Zone

As in some other areas of the house, it can help to divide your workspace into different areas based on the different tasks you need to do. This is more clear-cut if you're separating your sewing table and supplies from the desk where you do administrative tasks, but it can be as subtle as keeping receipts and other financial information together, or designating different file boxes for different projects. This keeps you organized in the obvious, physical sense—you know where to look for an ink cartridge if it's always in your printing zone. But it also helps you mentally feel on top of your tasks and ready to start your workday.

Rescue a Messed-Up Desktop

If your office desk is scratched, stained, or otherwise depressing to stare at all day, you can make it over in minutes. First, remove everything from your desktop. Then, get some contact paper. Choose a subtle, neutral color or pattern, like a pale marble, for a more sophisticated look. Carefully stick the contact paper to your desktop, starting at one corner and smoothing out any air bubbles as you go. An extra bonus to this quick and affordable project is that your desk will now be easy to wipe clean in case of a coffee spill!

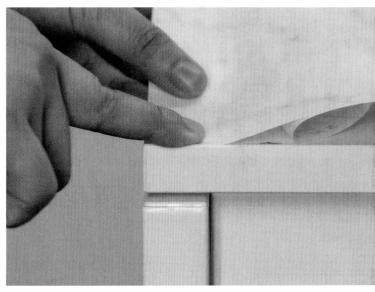
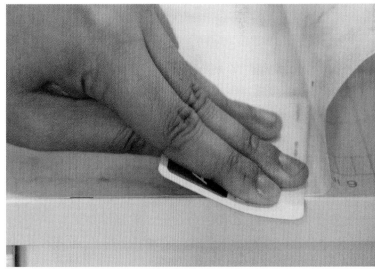

4 Ways to Carve Out a Cubicle in a Small Home

Even if you live and work in a small or unusually shaped home, or if your "office" is just the corner of a bedroom or studio apartment, you can still separate your workspace from the larger space. Here are some ways to do it:

1. Paint one accent wall, perhaps where your desk will go.

2. Use an attractive folding screen or colorful curtains.

3. Use a rug to block off a square of floor space.

4. Take advantage of a nook. If you're lucky enough to have an unused closet, strangely shaped hallway, or empty space under the stairs, a few adjustments can make it the most efficient little mini-office ever.

Maximize a Small Workspace

If you're dealing with a small workspace, it can be tricky to find storage solutions that fit. Here are a few ways to sneak extra storage space into your small home office:

- Choose a desk that utilizes vertical space, like a ladder desk or one with attached shelving above.

- Find desk accessories with multiple functions, like a lamp that's also a pen holder.

- Combine furniture to create storage. You could use a file cabinet or bookcase as the leg of a desk, or stack cubbies in a custom shape to make your storage fit your space.

- Look for vintage pieces. Older furniture, built before McMansions became the norm, is often smaller than modern pieces—and it can include creative storage, like in a rolltop desk.

Organize Your Other Desktop

Decluttered your physical desktop? Excellent. Now do your virtual one, because looking at a disorganized computer (or phone!) screen every time you sit down isn't helping your brain either.

Garage & Outdoor Spaces

Make the Most of What You've Got

Ah, the ***great outdoors***. It's beautiful, it's relaxing, and it needs to be cleaned and organized just like the rest of your home. These tips and tricks will help you get your outside areas in order, so you can spend more time planting flowers, sipping drinks, or whatever it is you like to do in your slice of the outdoors.

Make Your Own Patio Furniture Cleaner

If you sat outside all day and night, you'd start to feel pretty dirty pretty quick. It's no different for your patio furniture. To clean it, just pour ½ cup of white vinegar, 1 cup of club soda, 1 cup of dish soap, and 15 drops of essential oil into a spray bottle. Shake to mix. Spray the mixture onto chairs, tables, and other outdoor furniture, then scrub well with a scrub brush. Finally, wipe the suds off and polish with a clean cloth. (An extra tip: It's easier to clean outdoor furniture often, even when you're not using it, than waiting to tackle months of accumulated dirt on the first nice day of the year.)

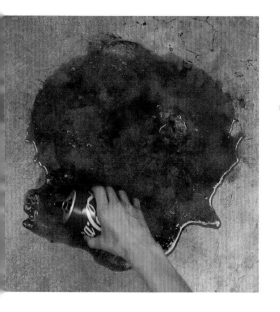

Remove Car Oil from Concrete

If a greasy, oily, ugly splotch is ruining the look of your garage floor, all you need to get it off is a scrub brush and some cola. Yup, the kind you drink. First, pour the soda directly onto the stain. Let it sit for 15 minutes while the carbonated water, phosphoric acid, and citric acid in the soda frees the grease from the concrete. (Just reapply if the soda runs down the driveway.) Then scrub the stain with a sturdy scrub brush. When you're done, hose off the area to clean. Repeat if necessary for older stains.

Remove Rust from Garden Tools

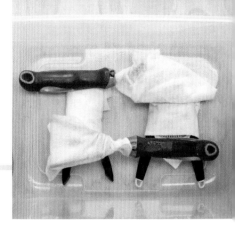

If your shovels, clippers, and other garden tools are coated with rust, all is not lost! Save them by filling a spray bottle with white vinegar and spray it all over the rusted metal. Then wrap the tools in paper towels, place them in a plastic bin, and spray again, saturating the paper towels. Let the tools sit like this for 2 hours, then remove the paper towels and scrub the metal with an old toothbrush. (Wear gloves to protect your hands!) Rinse the tools with water, then put them back in the bin and sprinkle baking soda over them. Add a few inches of water to the tub. Scrub the tools with the toothbrush again, then rinse and dry them. Finally, coat them with mineral oil. Good as new!

Clean Your Grill the Nontoxic Way

Shine up a greasy grill without harsh chemicals by cutting a lemon in half, pouring 2 table-spoons of salt on top, and scrubbing the grill grate with the salty citrus. Polish with a crumpled ball of aluminum foil, then rinse with soap and water.

Make Your Own Tool Belt DIY

Stop misplacing your garden tools by turning your old jeans into a clever utility belt. All you need is a pair of jeans you're about to get rid of, scissors, pins, and a needle and thread. First, cut off the legs and front of the jeans (hang on to the legs), leaving only the waistband and seat (which will become the front of your tool belt). To make extra pockets, cut off a few inches from the end of each pant leg, turn inside out, sew the raw hems, then turn them back the right way. Sew them to the front of your tool belt, just below the existing back (now front!) pockets of the jeans. Stick small tools in the four pockets and hang them on the belt loops.

Collect These Outdoor Cleaning Essentials

If you've just acquired a yard or other outdoor space after living your whole life without one, it can come as a shock. There's so much stuff involved! To start, here are the basic outdoor cleaning and organizing essentials:

- **Broom:** You'll need to sweep leaves and other debris from front steps and porch floors.

- **Rake:** Because leaves.

- **Lawn mower:** Because grass.

- **Shovel:** Because snow. (Unless you never get snow where you live, of course!)

- **Yard waste bags:** You don't want to throw out leaves, twigs, and other yard waste in plastic trash bags when it can be composted—in fact, doing so may not even be allowed where you live.

- **Work gloves:** Your hands deserve protection from scratches, blisters, poison ivy, fire ants, and other perils of the outside life.

- **Clippers or pruners:** There will always be some bush or branch that needs to be put in its place.

Dust a Window Screen

Ever wonder how to get that layer of dust off the outside of a window screen? You can clean it off quick with a lint roller. Genius, right?

Clean Your Outdoor Garbage Can

It may seem silly to clean a garbage can, but when you think about everything that's sat in there recently, you'll see why you need to. Follow these steps:

• Dump the can over and make sure it's truly empty.

• Rinse it inside and out with water. (This is easier to do with a hose, but you can just use a bucket.)

• Get our your favorite all-purpose cleaner—or use a bit of dish soap in water, or a mix of dish soap, water, and white vinegar. Spray it all over the can and scrub with a long-handled scrub brush or an old stiff-bristled broom.

• Rinse with water again, then leave the can with the lid open to dry fully. If it still stinks, pour in a few cups of white vinegar and let it soak for at least a few hours, or pour in some baking soda and leave it overnight, then rinse and dry again.

Clean Your Front Door

Your front door is often one of the first things people notice or really see in your home. If you neglect to clean the dust and grime that can build up on your front door, your visitors are getting an eyeful of dirt, pollen, and who knows what else.

To get aluminum or painted wooden doors looking sharp again, wipe using a rag and some mild soap and water, starting from the top and working your way down. If any tough stains remain, try a Magic Eraser. For a raw wooden door, dust the surface, then apply a wood oil. Polish metal fixtures like the doorknob and door knocker using a cleaner appropriate for the material, and clean glass windows or panels with a store-bought or homemade glass cleaner.

Get Sliding Doors Moving Smoothly Again

When too much of the outdoors gets into the crevices of your sliding door, sprinkle baking soda along the tracks and spread with an old toothbrush. Then spray white vinegar on top and let bubble. Lightly scrub with the toothbrush, then wipe with a rag and rinse with water to remove residue.

Make Your Own Garden Hose Storage

WHAT YOU NEED:

- Wooden bucket
- Drill and drill bits, including a hole saw bit
- Shallow planter that fits just inside the top rim of the bucket but doesn't fall in
- 2 (20-inch) pieces sisal rope
- Small potted succulents or other decorative outdoor objects

DIY

Is your garden hose lying on the ground, tripping passersby and tying itself in knots? This DIY container will keep your hose secure and add a cute decorative touch to your garden.

HOW TO DO IT:

1. Drill a hole through the side of the wooden bucket large enough for the hose to fit through.

2. Drill two smaller holes on each side of the shallow planter for the rope handles.

3. Thread the sisal rope pieces through the holes on both sides of the planter and knot them, creating two short handles.

4. Wind up the hose and place it in the bucket, threading the end through the hole in the side.

5. Set the planter "lid" on top of the bucket.

6. Fill the planter with plants or other objects.

7. Place near the outdoor tap so you can hook up the hose and water the lawn when you need to.

For an easier and faster version of this project, forgo the tools and rope and simply store the hose in the bucket, lifting the lid off without using handles!

Organize Your Garden Tools

How does your garden grow? Get it all in a row for good with these simple but super helpful garden organizing tips:

- Stir together sand and mineral oil in a bucket, then plant garden tools, metal side down, in the mixture to prevent rust and keep tools sharp. Keep the bucket covered or in the garage or shed to keep rain out.

- Organize seed packets in the plastic sleeves of an old photo album or CD case. Want extra credit? Alphabetize them.

- Store bulk seeds and fertilizers in snack dispensers. Pour out as much as you need, when you need, in perfectly controlled, mess-free portions!

- Remove plant tags from purchased plants, punch holes in the bottoms of the tags, and string them on a paper clip or key chain. Hang on a hook in your garden shed for a handy plant-care reference.

- Arrange your tools and gloves and hang with nails on a pegboard, then outline them with a marker so you'll always know what goes where.

- Store soil in airtight wheeled tubs to keep it fresh and bug-free while easily moving it around the yard.

- Keep a garden journal to jot down your backyard plans, tips and tricks you've learned, shopping lists, wish lists, garden rotations, and other relevant info.

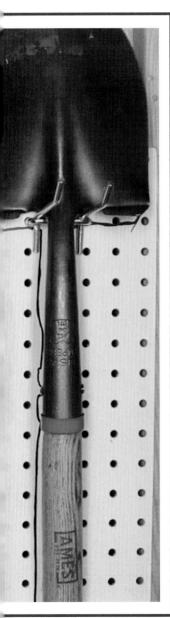

Zone Out

Just as in other multi-use areas of your home, it can be useful to think of your outdoor spaces in terms of zones and set up furniture and storage accordingly. This is especially true if different people gravitate to different spots—for instance, the kids play in one corner of the yard where their toys are stored, the artist in the family uses the shed as a studio, and the resident gardener is in charge of the raised beds. Creating zones can help you organize your outdoor areas, make it easier to clean up after a day of outside activities, and let you maintain a neat environment all the time.

Rethink Your Shed

It doesn't take much to convert a shed into an epic playhouse for kids, or the ultimate doghouse for a furry friend. If you entertain often, your shed could become an outdoor bar. If you crave solitude, a shed could be a cozy office, studio space, or reading nook. A shed can take backyard camping to backyard glamping, or help you realize your dream of raising chickens.

Store Chemicals Safely

If you store any chemicals in your garage or shed, lock them up securely so children and animals can't get to them. Also, keep products in their original containers—or label homemade stuff clearly—and make sure anything that needs to be kept in a ventilated space is stored properly.

Assemble Outdoor Activity Caddies

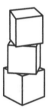

When you like to do different activities outside but you can't store the associated materials outside, make your life easier by filling a few plastic shower caddies with all your outdoor things. For example, stock a caddy with:

- **Gardening tools:** Sunscreen, hat, and gloves

- **Entertaining supplies:** Casual table settings and utensils

- **Reading materials:** Sunglasses, beach towel, and books or magazines

- **Toys for kids:** Sidewalk chalk, bubbles, and jump rope

- **Dog-walking gear:** Poop collection bags and a leash

    Store your caddies inside, somewhere near the door, so you can just grab one and go.

Make Sure Your Doormat Actually Collects Dirt

That front doormat with the snarky greeting in a cutesy font? It may be amusing, but it's useless if it can't actually scrub mud and dirt off your shoes. Make sure any mat you buy is functional and durable and not just decorative. One of the easiest ways to clean your house less frequently is to bring less dirt into it!

Beware Standing Water

Not only does standing water leave stains and make things look ugly, but it can also be a breeding ground for bugs. When rainwater collects in your flowerpots, or on unused patio furniture, take a second to dump it out before it attracts mosquitoes.

Keep Track of Your Extra Key

Need to surreptitiously store an extra key outside? Glue an unassuming rock to the lid of a pill bottle. Then pop the key in the bottle, close the lid, and bury the bottle in the yard so only the rock rests on top of the soil.

Waterproof All the Things

Even if your balcony or porch is covered, rain or snow *will* eventually find a way to sneak in. Don't buy any furniture, pillows, curtains, or decorations that aren't weatherproof. Waterproof items still look great and will be so much easier to keep clean.

4 Ways to Use PVC Pipe to Organize Your Shed or Garage

Are tools taking over your shed or garage? Organize them neatly along one wall with these simple PVC pipe hacks:

1. Keep handled tools in place using wooden planks and a few 2-inch PVC pipes. First, attach two wooden planks horizontally to the wall. Cut PVC pipe into short sections and glue them vertically to the planks. Insert tool handles into the pipe sections.

2. Organize screwdrivers by drilling multiple holes through a 1-inch PVC pipe. Attach the pipe to the wall horizontally, with the holes pointing up and down, and place screwdrivers in the holes.

3. Keep rolls of tape tidy with a ¾-inch PVC pipe and paracord. Thread the doubled-up cord through the pipe, tie the loose ends, and hang both ends of the cord from two nails in the wall. Store tape rolls on the pipe.

4. Organize drills with a plank of wood and some 3-inch PVC pipes. Cut the pipes to fit the length of your drills, then cut out a rectangle on one side of each. Attach sections of pipe side by side to a wooden plank, with the rectangular cutouts facing out. Attach the plank to the wall with the pipes facing down and the cutouts facing out. Then slide your drills into the pipes for easy access. (The plank can also function as a shelf!)

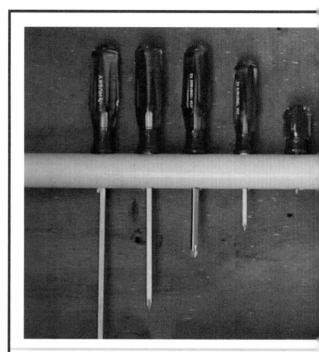

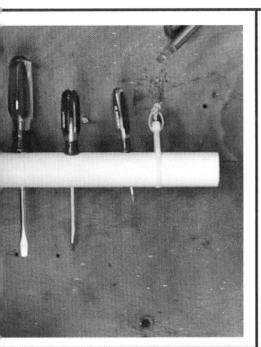

Increase Garage Storage Space

If you think your garage is only for your car, think again: Installing overhead storage racks can make even a small garage a potential storage bonanza. That vertical space could hold a lot of items you don't need to access regularly.

Repurpose a Pallet

Old pallets aren't just for firewood or the recycling bin. See if you can get one for free or nearly free from a local store, then hang one on an interior garage or shed wall and use S-hooks to hang tools from the slats.

Use Those Walls

Save space in a small garage or shed by storing as much as you can on wall-mounted racks. To start, install a tool rack to organize everything from snow shovels and ladders to brooms and smaller tools for gardening and cleaning.

Roll with It

When it comes to garage or shed storage, the only container more practical than a giant plastic tub is a giant plastic tub with wheels on it.

Extra Spaces

Top-Shelf Closets

"Extra spaces" are those frequently neglected rooms, closets, and halls, those places you always say you'll totally **clean and organize**—someday. This chapter contains a whole bunch of tips and hacks to help you finally get **your extra spaces** as neat and clean as the more obvious rooms in your home.

4 Creative Small Entryway Space Savers

Even if you don't have one of those palatial entryways big enough to be rented out as a separate apartment in some cities, you can still make your space both organized and pretty. Try one or more of the following:

1. If your entry is too small for a large console table, try a folding TV table. That's plenty of space to hold essentials like outgoing mail, a dish for catching keys and jewelry, and even nonessentials like a little vase of flowers.

2. If any sort of table is impossible, install a floating shelf rack instead. Make it more versatile by adding hooks to the ledge for keys.

3. Instead of a fancy bench, put a small round stool in the entryway. Even better, make it an ottoman with a lid, adding storage space for scarves and gloves.

4. If you have wall space, take advantage of it by hanging an accordion rack to hang everything from bags to scarves to a little outgoing letter basket. Or hang individual hooks or knobs, gallery wall–style.

Keep These Essentials in Your Entryway

Whether your entryway is a wide hallway, a mudroom, or a wall next to your apartment door, there are a few things you need to make it comfortable and functional. You don't want to put too much stuff in an entryway—that will just be harder to keep clean and neat—but you do want to add some form of these five things:

1. **Bowl for keys:** It doesn't need to be a bowl specifically; a dish, stand, tray, or wall-mounted organizer will do just fine.

2. **Console table or bench to hold larger items:** Your entryway is going to become a magnet for bags, mail, packages, and things you need to remember to take with you tomorrow. A piece of furniture—or at least a cubby or shelf or two—will keep these items organized for you.

3. **Rug or mat to wipe your shoes:** Since most people take shoes off here, you might also want to add a place to put shoes—even if it's just temporary.

4. **Closet or other place for outerwear:** This could also be a coat tree, a coat rack, or hooks. Or you could combine a few storage solutions, such as a rack of hooks for coats and a woven basket for hats and mittens.

5. **Mirror:** This one isn't 100 percent essential, but you might find you like having at least a small mirror somewhere near the front door so you can quickly check your look before you step out.

Convert
Storage Cubes Into
an Entryway Bench

WHAT YOU NEED:

- Cube organizer (the height will be the length of your bench)
- Measuring tape
- 1-inch thick MDF board
- High-density foam (at least 1 inch thick, but can be much thicker if you prefer)
- Cotton batting
- Fabric
- Staple gun with staples
- Drill, 6 (1$\frac{1}{2}$-inch) screws, and a drill bit (optional)

One clever and functional option in an entryway is to turn an open cube organizer into a bench that doubles as storage cubbies. And it's surprisingly easy to do!

HOW TO DO IT:

1. Turn the organizer onto its side and measure the length and width. Cut the MDF board and foam to the same length and width as the organizer.

2. Stack the MDF board directly on top of the organizer, and the foam on top of the MDF board. Cut cotton batting large enough to cover both the board and the foam with approximately 4 extra inches on each side.

3. Cut the fabric slightly larger than the cotton batting. Wrap and fold the edges of the batting and fabric under the MDF board as if you're making a bed.

4. Flip the MDF board over, then tightly fold over the corners of the fabric and batting and staple them to the MDF board. Staple the fabric and batting all down the middle as well. Flip the seat cushion back over so that the fabric is facing upward.

5. Optional: If you like, you can attach the seat cushion to the bench by drilling from under the organizer and into the MDF board.

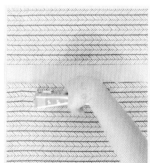

Make an Entryway Boot Station

It takes only a few rainy or snowy days to turn the cleanest entryway into a mud puddle full of boots. Stop a dirty, drippy situation before it starts with this easy DIY project:

- Cover the bottom of a large tray with flat stones to improve drainage, and put it on the floor in your entryway.

- Place a boot scraper on a mat on the floor next to your tray.

- Nearby, place a small basket holding a container of disinfectant wipes (to wipe down dirty soles) and a spray bottle filled with a mix of equal parts water and white vinegar (to eliminate odors inside shoes). If your boots sometimes get coated with road salt, add a small jar filled with cotton balls, and another containing 1 tablespoon of white vinegar mixed with 1 cup of water. Rub leather or sheepskin boots with a saturated cotton ball, then wipe with a dry cloth to remove those annoying salty splotches.

- Attach two hooks to the wall above your boot station to hold an umbrella or coats.

- If you have room, add a chair or stool where you can sit down to remove and clean your footwear. Even better, choose a bench with storage space underneath to stash your boots once they're clean and dry.

5 Ways to Maximize Space in a Small Closet

If you're stuck with a tiny or inconveniently shaped linen or hall closet, you might have to get help from some organizing products before you can really sort out your storage. Here are some ideas:

1. Use multiple small, clear organizers. Small items like bottles of nail polish, hair clips, and pill bottles fit well in these. These organizers can be rearranged to fit on differently sized shelves and make it easy to see what you have.

2. Add shelves where you need them. Look for extra space up high, near the ceiling, even if it means that you store infrequently used items there and retrieve them with a step stool.

3. Think about putting a low shelf just above the floor. Sometimes adding a second level here means you can store twice as much stuff.

4. Install a tension rod or two. In a closet with shelves, a rod can sometimes add more, or a different type of, extra storage; in a small but deep closet, you might be able to add a second rod behind an existing one.

5. Use vacuum bags for blankets. Taking the air out of the bags greatly reduces the amount of space they take up.

Declutter Your Hall Closet

Cleaning out a front or hall closet can be overwhelming because of the amount of stuff that accumulates here. Here's how to tackle the job:

- Take everything out and clean the closet itself.

- Evaluate all the items you've removed. Think about whether you still like, need, and/or use each item, and put everything you no longer want in a bag to dispose of or donate.

- Decide if what's left actually belongs in this closet. Consider whether this is the most logical place for it—is this where you would naturally come looking for it?

- Put items that are staying here back—neatly—and enjoy your newly organized closet.

Customize Your Closet

No, you don't need to buy or build one of those complex closet systems. You just need to think of how the closet setup would be most convenient for you, and then (within the restrictions of budget and rental agreements) change it however you want.

For example, if your hall closet has a rod for hanging coats, that doesn't mean you have to use it! If it makes more sense for you, hang your coats on wall-mounted hooks, take the rod out, and install shelves in that closet. Or take the door off and put a table, mirror, and boot tray in it to expand your entryway. Don't let those closets tell you how to live.

Double Up How You Use Certain Spaces

It's easy to fall into the trap of thinking a room or closet has to have a single purpose. But if you want a guest room that's also a photography studio or a gym, then go for it!

Transform a Hallway Into a Storage Space

If you don't have much in the way of storage spaces like closets or spare rooms, you might have another sneaky organization option: a hallway. There are all kinds of small ways you can dress up a hall in organization-friendly decor, and they can add up to some serious storage space.

• Hang hooks or a coat rack on the wall to hang outerwear and bags.

• Add a bench with a hidden—or not so hidden—storage compartment.

• Install some ever-versatile floating shelves, or place a narrow bookshelf or console table along one wall.

A hallway near the door can function as an entryway if you don't technically have one, and a hallway near bedrooms and bathrooms can do the job of a linen closet. To make it work, use walls as much as possible, and choose furniture that doesn't stick out too far from the walls.

5 Steps to Decluttering a Storage Space

Moving? Spring cleaning? On a decluttering kick? Overwhelmed by a storage area that hasn't been cleaned out since about the Cretaceous period? Here are some tips to help you wrangle the clutter:

1. Break it down. If the room is large, you might want to split this task over several days, and even in a smaller space, like a closet; dealing with one shelf before moving to the next will give shape to the process.

2. Look through every box and into every corner. You might assume you know what's in there—or you might not want to know—but life and storage bins are full of surprises.

3. Be ready to let go of items. Come prepared with trash bags for items you're tossing, recycling, selling, or giving away.

4. Be real. If you know deep down you're never going to use those craft supplies or wear those clothes from high school, let them go.

5. Label everything. When you've decided what you're keeping, store it neatly and label it thoroughly.

Keep Your Hobby Room Organized

If you have a space you're using as a studio, gym, practice area, or reading nook, have fun setting up a space dedicated to an activity you love. So how can you keep this extra space neat? First, remind yourself that this space has a specific purpose. Don't add things that have nothing to do with that, just because they physically fit in the room. Second, don't haphazardly fill your gym with equipment or your library with books just because you can; buy and store only what you're really going to use.

Make Your Spare Room Work for You

Sometimes a spare room gets cluttered simply because you don't know what else to do with it; if you don't need it as a guest room or a home office, it's tempting to just sort of shove all your extra stuff in there and close the door. To get a room like this in order, first, you have to decide what it's for. The possibilities are almost endless, but think about making your extra room into an art studio, craft space, home gym, library, or a dedicated place to practice music, do yoga, or work on your individual hobby or passion projects.

And if you really don't have space elsewhere, you can make at least part of your spare room into a storage area. Keep it organized by sticking to a fixed number of shelves or clearly dividing the room into sections.

Store Your Stuff Safely

If you're storing stuff in a basement or attic, use tubs or bins that will protect your things from any exposure to hot, cold, or damp conditions. (And mice, eek!) Also, consider storing particularly delicate items elsewhere.

Decide What to Store Where

When you have multiple closets and storage spaces, it helps to make a clear distinction about what kind of stuff you store where. In general, you want the things you use most often to go where you can most easily reach them, and the things you use only occasionally (or rarely) to go in less accessible areas. For example, keep sheets and towels in the linen closet and holiday decorations in the basement. Within a space, put things you use less often on a high shelf or toward the back, and keep items you'll need soon front and center.

Another thing to consider is where you use stuff. If you have the option, store items close to where you'll need them—one obvious example being coats in the front closet, near the door.

Label Everything You Store

Labels can make your life easier in pretty much any room, but they're especially helpful in storage spaces. You may feel certain you're going to remember what's in there, but don't kid yourself. Label everything. You'll thank yourself later.

Manage Holiday & Seasonal Decor

Holidays are supposed to be fun, but packing and storing holiday decorations can be anything but. Here are some simple tips that you'll be glad you followed when it's time to find all this stuff again next year.

- Use Bubble Wrap to protect small, fragile items like ceramic ghost figurines.

- Stash smaller decor items inside larger ones—like fall candleholders in a big plastic pumpkin—for extra protection (and to take up less space).

- Wind strings of fairy lights around wire clothes hangers to keep them from tangling.

- Store decorations made of cloth, paper, or any soft material, like faux cobwebs, in zip-top plastic bags. Leaving the top open, roll to squeeze out excess air before sealing.

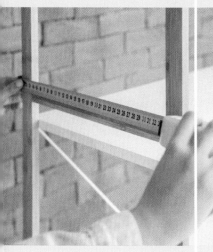

5 Common Storage Mistakes to Avoid

Everyone makes mistakes, and when it comes to organizing storage spaces—closets, basements, attics, any room with shelves—everyone tends to make the *same* mistakes. When you're trying to tidy your storage areas, be on the lookout for these storage-sabotaging errors:

1. **Buying organizers that come in sets with a small, medium, and large:** They look practical in the store, but in reality, most household items—and most shelves—are basically medium-sized. There are exceptions, of course, but if you always end up with one container that's too big or too small to be useful, your situation is not one of them.

2. **Buying organizing products before measuring:** Even if you're a good judge of space, you only have to be $1/4$ inch off to render your brand-new storage bins useless. Measure your closets or shelves before committing to any boxes or baskets.

3. **Buying dozens of identical storage containers:** This plan can sometimes be fine—if you're storing many things that are all the same size on shelves that are all the same distance apart. But more often, you'll want some variety to accommodate all your things.

4. **Cramming stuff in too tight:** Even if it's technically organized, a closet that's so packed that you can't easily grab what you need isn't a functional storage solution. Either purge some stuff or find additional storage space.

5. **Storing everything forever:** Even if you have the space, failing to declutter will eventually lead to an organization nightmare.

Find the Best Storage Options for Your Space

Go to any home store and you'll find aisles of baskets, bins, and tubs. They all look like they can magically organize your entire life, but which ones are the best? Here are the pros and cons of some common organizing containers.

- **Plastic tubs:** They are sturdy, have lids, and can hold a serious amount of stuff. They're great for longer-term storage in attics and basements, where dampness or bugs are possibilities. But they're not the cutest, so they're best for storage areas that aren't always visible.

- **Baskets:** They come in a variety of sizes, colors, and patterns, and can look attractive. But they won't protect from the elements, and they're usually not great for stacking.

- **Canvas boxes:** They're nice options in closets and open shelving, the ones with lids can be stacked, and they often have space for a label. However, they're not the sturdiest, and they can be damaged by liquids.

- **Soft plastic zippered bags:** Ideal for storing off-season clothes, these can be wedged into tight spaces.

Make Open Storage Look Organized

When you're trying to organize a storage area that can't be hidden, like a corner of a spare room, the space can look tacky and/or messy in a hurry. Here are some tricks for getting open storage space to actually *look* organized.

- **Use simple, matching shelves.** This strategy keeps the look streamlined and uniform so it doesn't attract any more attention than it needs to.

- **Go with opaque organizers.** Clear bins can be very helpful in certain situations, but when your storage is more open, the sight of all that stuff reads, visually, as clutter.

- **Choose containers in one color or a narrow range of colors.** When you glance over at a shelf and see row upon row of black boxes or flax baskets, it instantly registers as intentional and organized.

- **Make sure your organizers are the right sizes.** You don't want anything you're storing to stick out of the top of a basket, or force the lid off a plastic tub.

Index